EYEWITNESS TRAVEL
SPANISH
V I S U A L
PHRASE BOOK

DK
A Dorling Kindersley Book

LONDON, NEW YORK, MELBOURNE,
MUNICH, DELHI

Senior Editor Angela Wilkes
Art Editor Silke Spingies
Production Editor Lucy Baker
Production Controller Inderjit Bhullar
Managing Editor Julie Oughton
Managing Art Editor Christine Keilty
Reference Publisher Jonathan Metcalf
Art Director Bryn Walls

Produced for Dorling Kindersley by
SP Creative Design
Editor Heather Thomas
Designer Rolando Ugolino

Language content for Dorling Kindersley
by First Edition Translations Ltd,
Cambridge, UK
Translator Elena Urena
Typesetting Essential Typesetting

First published in Great Britain in 2008
by Dorling Kindersley Limited,
80 Strand, London WC2R 0RL

A Penguin Company

2 4 6 8 10 9 7 5 3 1

A CIP catalogue record for this book is
available from the British Library

ISBN: 978-1-4053-3107-4

Printed by Leo Paper China

Discover more at
www.dk.com

CONTENTS

INTRODUCTION

This book provides all the key words and phrases you are
likely to need in everyday situations. It is grouped into
themes, and key phrases are broken down into short
sections, to help you build a wide variety of sentences.
A lot of the vocabulary is illustrated to make it easy to
remember, and "You may hear" boxes feature questions
you are likely to hear. At the back of the book there is a
menu guide, listing about 500 food terms, and a 2,000-
word two-way dictionary. Numbers and the most useful
phrases are listed on the jacket flaps for quick reference.

Nouns and adjectives

All Spanish nouns (words for things, people, and ideas)
are masculine or feminine. The gender of nouns is shown
by the word used for '"the": **el** (masculine singular) and
la (feminine singular). The words for "the" before plurals
are **los** (masculine) and **las** (feminine).

Adjectives

Most Spanish adjectives change endings according to
whether they describe a masculine or feminine, singular or
plural word. In this book the singular masculine form is
shown, followed by the alternative feminine ending:
I'm married   **Soy casado/a**

"You"

There are two ways of saying "you" in Spanish: **usted**
(polite) and **tú** (familiar). In this book we have used
usted, as it is normally used with people you don't know.

Verbs

Verbs usually change depending on whether they are in
the singular or plural. Where this happens, you will see the
singular form of the verb followed by the plural form:
Where is/are…?   **¿Dónde está/están…?**

Pronunciation guide

Below each Spanish word or phrase in this book, you will find a pronunciation guide. Read it as if it were English and you should be understood, but remember that it is only a guide and for the best results you should listen to and mimic native speakers. Some Spanish sounds are different from those in English and this book teaches European Spanish, which differs in pronunciation from Latin American Spanish. Take note of how the letters below are pronounced.

a like a in cap

c before a, o, and u, like k in kite
before i and e, like th in thin

e like e in wet
at the end of a word, like ay in may

g before a, o, and u, like g in got
before e and i, like ch in the Scottish word loch

h silent

i like ee in keep

ie in the middle of a word, like y in yes

j like ch in the Scottish word loch

ll like y in yes

ñ like ni in onion

o like oa in boat

q like k in king

r trilled like a Scottish r , especially at the beginning of a word and when double r

u like oo in boot

v like a soft b

z like th in thin

ESSENTIALS

In this section, you will find the essential words and useful phrases that you will need in Spain for basic everyday talk and situations. You should be aware of cultural differences when you are addressing Spanish people, and remember that they tend to be quite formal with strangers, often using the polite *usted* form of address, rather than the more familiar *tú* for "you" and shaking hands. Use the formal form with people you don't know.

GREETINGS

Hello	Hola *ohlah*
Good evening	Buenas tardes *bwenas tardais*
Good night	Buenas noches *bwenas nochais*
Goodbye	Adiós *adyos*
Hi/bye!	¡Hola/adiós! *ohlah/adyos*
Pleased to meet you	Encantado de conocerle *enkantadoh day konotherlay*
How are you?	¿Cómo está? *komoh estah*
Fine, thanks	Bien, gracias *byen grathyas*
You're welcome	De nada *day nadah*
My name is …	Me llamo… *may yamoh*
What's your name?	¿Cómo se llama? *komoh say yamah*
What's his/her name?	¿Cómo se llama él/ella? *komoh say yamah el/eyah*
This is …	Éste es… *estay es*
Nice to meet you	Mucho gusto *moochoh goostoh*
See you tomorrow	Hasta mañana *astah manyanah*
See you soon	Hasta pronto *astah prontoh*

SMALL TALK

Yes/no	Sí/no *see/noh*
Please	Por favor *por fabor*
Thank you (very much)	(Muchas) gracias *moochas grathyas*
You're welcome	De nada *day nadah*
OK/fine	Bien *byen*
Pardon?	¿Perdón? *pairdon*
Excuse me	Disculpe *deeskoolpay*
Sorry	Lo siento *loh syentoh*
I don't know	No lo sé *noh loh say*
I don't understand	No le entiendo *noh lay aintyendoh*
Could you repeat that?	¿Puede repetir? *pweday repeteer*
I don't speak Spanish	No hablo español *noh ahbloh espanyol*
Do you speak English?	¿Habla usted inglés? *ahblah oosted eenglais*
What is the Spanish for...?	¿Cómo se dice...en español? *komoh say deethay...en espanyol*
What's that?	¿Qué es eso? *kay es esoh*
What's that called?	¿Cómo se llama eso? *komoh say yamah esoh*
Can you tell me...	¿Puede decirme...? *pweday detheermay*

TALKING ABOUT YOURSELF

I'm from...	Soy de... *soy day*
I'm...	Soy... *soy*
...English	...inglés/inglesa *...eenglais/eenglaisah*
...American	...estadounidense *...aistadoh-oonydensay*
...Canadian	...canadiense *...kanadyensay*
...Australian	...australiano/a *...aoostralyanoh/ah*
...single	...soltero/a *...solteroh/ah*
...married	...casado/a *...kasadoh/ah*
...divorced	...divorciado/a *...deeborthyadoh/ah*
I am...years old	Tengo...años *taingoh...anyos*
I have...	Tengo... *taingoh*
...a boyfriend/girlfriend	...novio/novia *...nobyo/nobya*
...two children	...dos hijos *...dos eehos*

You may hear...

- **¿De dónde es usted?**
  day donday es oosted
  Where are you from?

- **¿Está casado?**
  estuh kasadoh
  Are you married?

- **¿Tiene hijos?**
  tyenay eehos
  Do you have children?

SOCIALIZING

Do you live here?	¿Vive aquí? *beebay ahkee*
Where do you live?	¿Dónde vive? *donday beebay*
I am here...	Estoy aquí... *estoy ahkee*
...on holiday	...de vacaciones *day bakathyonais*
...on business	...en viaje de negocios *en beeyahay day negothyos*
I'm a student	Soy estudiante *soy estoodyantay*
I work in...	Trabajo en... *trabahoh en*
I am retired	Estoy jubilado *estoy hoobeeladoh*
Can I have...	¿Me da... *may dah*
...your telephone number?	...su número de teléfono? *soo noomeroh day telefonoh*
...your email address?	...su dirección de email? *soo deerekthyon day eemaeel*
It doesn't matter	No importa *noh eemportah*
Cheers	Salud *salood*
Do you mind if I smoke?	¿Le importa que fume? *lay eemportah kay foomay*
I don't drink/smoke	No bebo alcohol/no fumo *noh beboh alkol/noh foomoh*
Are you alright?	¿Se encuentra bien? *say enkwentrah byen*
I'm OK	Estoy bien *estoy byen*

LIKES AND DISLIKES

I like/love…	Me gusta/encanta *may goostah/enkantah*
I don't like…	No me gusta… *noh may goostah*
I hate…	Detesto… *daytestoh*
I quite/really like…	Me gusta bastante/mucho… *may goostah bastantay/moochoh*
Don't you like it?	¿No te gusta? *noh tay goostah*
I would like…	Quisiera *keesyerah*
I'd like this one/that one	Quisiera éste/ése *keesyerah estay/esay*
My favourite is…	Mi preferido es… *mee prefereedoh es*
I prefer…	Prefiero… *prefyeroh*
It's delicious	Está delicioso *estah dayleethyosoh*
What would you like to do?	¿Qué le gustaría hacer? *kay lay goostarya ahthair*
I don't mind	Me da igual *may dah ygwal*

You may hear...

- ¿Qué hace?
  kay ahthay
  What do you do?

- ¿Está de vacaciones?
  estah day bakathyonais
  Are you on holiday?

- ¿Le gusta…?
  lay goostah
  Do you like…?

DAYS OF THE WEEK

What day is it today?	¿Qué día es hoy? *kay deeyah es oi*
Sunday	domingo *domeengoh*
Monday	lunes *loonais*
Tuesday	martes *martais*
Wednesday	miércoles *myerkolais*
Thursday	jueves *hooebes*
Friday	viernes *byernais*
Saturday	sábado *sabadoh*
today	hoy *oi*
tomorrow	mañana *manyanah*
yesterday	ayer *ayair*
in…days	dentro de…días *daintro day…deeyas*

THE SEASONS

primavera
preemabairah
spring

verano
bairanoh
summer

MONTHS

January	enero *aineroh*
February	febrero *febrairoh*
March	marzo *marthoh*
April	abril *ahbreel*
May	mayo *mayoh*
June	junio *hoonyoh*
July	julio *hoolyoh*
August	agosto *agostoh*
September	septiembre *saiptyembray*
October	octubre *oktoobray*
November	noviembre *nobyembray*
December	diciembre *deethyembray*

otoño
otonyoh
autumn

invierno
eenbyernoh
winter

TELLING THE TIME

What time is it?	¿Qué hora es? *kay ohrah es*
It's nine o'clock	Son las nueve *son las nwaibay*
...in the morning	...de la mañana *day lah manyanah*
...in the afternoon	...de la tarde *day lah tarday*
...in the evening	...de la noche *day lah nochay*

la una en punto
lah oonah en poontoh
one o'clock

la una y diez
lah oonah ee deeyaith
ten past one

la una y cuarto
lah oonah ee kwartoh
quarter past one

la una y veinte
lah oonah ee baintay
twenty past one

la una y media
lah oonah ee medya
half past one

las dos menos cuarto
las dos mainos kwartoh
quarter to two

las dos menos diez
las dos mainos deeyaith
ten to two

las dos en punto
las dos en poontoh
two o'clock

It's midday/midnight	Es mediodía/medianoche *es medyodeeyah/ medyanochay*
second	el segundo *el saigoondoh*
minute	el minuto *el meenootoh*
hour	la hora *lah ohrah*
a quarter of an hour	un cuarto de hora *oon kwartoh day ohrah*
half an hour	media hora *medya ohrah*
three-quarters of an hour	tres cuartos de hora *trais kwartos day ohrah*
late	tarde *tarday*
early	temprano *taimpranoh*
soon	pronto *prontoh*
What time does it start?	¿A qué hora empieza? *ah kay ohrah empyethah*
What time does it finish?	¿A qué hora termina? *ah kay ohrah termeenah*

You may hear...

- **Hasta luego.**
  astah lwegoh
  See you later.

- **Llega temprano.**
  yegah taimpranoh
  You're early.

- **Llega tarde.**
  yegah tarday
  You're late.

THE WEATHER

What's the forecast?	¿Cuál es la previsión del tiempo? *kwal es lah praibeesyon dail tyempoh*
What's the weather like?	¿Qué tiempo hace? *kay tyempoh ahthay*
It's...	Hace... *ahthay*
...good	...bueno *bwenoh*
...bad	...mal tiempo *mal tyempoh*
...warm	...una buena temperatura *oonah bwenah temperatoorah*
...hot	...calor *kalor*
...cold	...frío *freeyoh*

Hace sol
ahthay sol
It's sunny

Está lloviendo
estah yobyendoh
It's raining

Está nublado
estah noobladoh
It's cloudy

Hay tormenta
ah-ee tormaintah
It's stormy

What's the temperature?	¿Qué temperatura hace? *kay temperatoorah ahthay*
It's ...degrees	...grados *grahdos*
It's a beautiful day	Hace un día precioso *ahthay oon deeyah prethyosoh*
The weather's changing	El tiempo está cambiando *el tyempoh estah kambyandoh*
Is it going to get colder/hotter?	¿Empezará a hacer más frío/calor? *empetharah ah ahthair mas freeyoh/kalor*
It's cooling down	Hace más frío *ahthay mas freeyoh*
Is it going to freeze?	¿Helará? *ehlahrah*

Está nevando
estah naibandoh
It's snowing

Hay hielo
ah-ee yeloh
It's icy

Hay niebla
ah-ee nyeblah
It's misty

Hace viento
ahthay byentoh
It's windy

GETTING AROUND

Spain has a good road and motorway network
if you are travelling around the country by car.
Spanish trains are fast and punctual, linking the
major towns and cities. The high-speed AVE service
links the capital Madrid with Seville in the south.
You can also travel, of course, by taxi, bus, coach
or plane. In the cities of Madrid, Barcelona and
Bilbao, the *Metro* (underground railway) is a quick
and easy way of getting around.

ASKING WHERE THINGS ARE

Excuse me, please	Disculpe, por favor *deeskoolpay por fabor*
Where is...	¿Dónde está... *donday estah*
...the town centre?	...el centro? *el thentroh*
...the railway station?	...la estación de tren? *lah estathyon day tren*
...the cash machine?	...el cajero automático? *el kaheroh ah-ootomateekoh*
How do I get to...?	¿Cómo se va a...? *komoh say bah ah*
I'm going to...	Voy a... *Boy ah*
I'm looking for...	Busco... *booskoh*
I'm lost	Me he perdido *may perdeedoh*
Is it near?	¿Está cerca? *estah therkah*
Is there a...nearby?	¿Hay un...por aquí cerca? *ah-ee oon...por ahkee therkah*
Is it far?	¿Está lejos? *estah lehos*
How far is...	¿Queda muy lejos... *kedah mooy lehos*
...the town hall?	...el ayuntamiento? *el ayoontamyentoh*
...the market?	...el mercado? *el merkadoh*
Can I walk there?	¿Se puede ir andando? *say pweday eer andandoh*
Do I have to drive?	¿Hay que ir en coche? *ah-ee kay eer en kochay*

CAR RENTAL

Where is the car rental desk?	¿Dónde está el mostrador de alquiler de coches? *donday estah el mostrador day alkeelair day kochais*
I want to hire…	Quiero alquilar… *kyero alkeelar*
…a car	…un coche *oon kochay*
…a bicycle	…una bicicleta *oonah beetheekletah*

el turismo
el tooreesmoh
saloon car

el coche de cinco puertas
el kochay day theenkoh pwertas
hatchback

la moto
lah motoh
motorbike

la vespa
lah baispah
scooter

la bicicleta de montaña
lah beetheekletah day montanyah
mountain bike

for…days	para…días *parah…deeyas*
for a week	para una semana *parah oonah semanah*

for the weekend	para el fin de semana *parah el feen day semanah*
I'd like…	Lo quisiera… *loh keesyerah*
…an automatic	…automático *ah-ootomateekoh*
…a manual	…manual *manooal*
Has it got air conditioning?	¿Tiene aire acondicionado? *tyenay ah-yray ahkondeethyonadoh*
Should I return it with a full tank?	¿Tengo que devolverlo con el depósito lleno? *taingoh kay debolberloh kon el daiposeetoh yenoh*
Here's my driving licence	Aquí tiene mi carné de conducir *ahkee tyenay mee karneh day kondootheer*
Can I hire a…	¿Puedo alquilar un…? *pwedoh alkeelar oon*

la silla para niños
lah seeyah parah neenyos
child seat

el casco de ciclismo
el kaskoh day theekleesmoh
cycling helmet

el candado
el kandadoh
lock

la mancha
lah manchah
pump

DRIVING

Is this the road to...?	¿Es ésta la carretera que lleva a...? *es estah lah karreterah kay yebah ah*
Where is the nearest garage?	¿Dónde está el garaje más cercano? *donday estah el garahay mas therkanoh*
I'd like...	Póngame... *pongamay*
...some petrol	...gasolina *gasoleenah*
...40 litres of unleaded	...cuarenta litros de gasolina sin plomo *kwahrentah lee-tros day gasoleenah seen plomoh*
...30 litres of diesel	...treinta litros de diesel *traintah lee-tros day deeyaysail*
Fill it up, please	Lleno, por favor *yenoh por fabor*
Where do I pay?	¿Dónde hay que pagar? *donday ah-y kay pagar*
The pump number is...	El número del surtidor es... *el noomeroh dail soorteedor es*
Can I pay by credit card?	¿Se puede pagar con tarjeta de crédito? *say pweday pagar kon tarhetah day kredeetoh*

la gasolinera
lah gasoleenerah
petrol station

Please can you check...	Por favor, compruebe... *por fabor komprwebay*
...the oil	...el aceite *el ahthaytay*
...the tyre pressure	...la presión de las ruedas *lah presyon day las rwedas*

PARKING

Is there a car park nearby?	¿Hay un aparcamiento por aquí cerca? *ah-ee oon ahparkamyentoh por ahkee therkah*
Can I park here?	¿Se puede aparcar aquí? *say pweday ahparkar ahkee*
How long can I park for?	¿Cuánto tiempo se puede aparcar? *kwanto tyempoh say pweday ahparkar*
How much does it cost?	¿Cuánto cuesta? *kwanto kwestah*
How much is it...	¿Cuánto es... *kwanto es*
...per hour?	...por hora? *por ohrah*
...per day?	...por día? *por deeyah*
...overnight?	...por toda la noche? *por todah lah nochay*

la silla infantil para el coche
lah seeyah eenfanteel parah el kochay
child seat

THE CAR

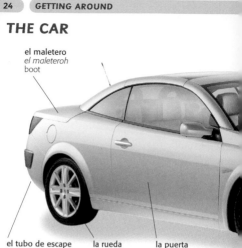

el maletero
el maleteroh
boot

el tubo de escape
el tooboh day eskapay
exhaust

la rueda
lah rwedah
wheel

la puerta
lah pwertah
door

INSIDE THE CAR

el cinturón de seguridad
el theentooron day segooreedad
seat belt

el cierre de la puerta
el thyerray day lah pwertah
door lock

el asiento trasero
el ahsyentoh traseroh
back seat

el asiento delantero
el ahsyaintoh dailanteroh
front seat

el parabrisas
el parabreesas
windscreen

el capó
el kapoh
bonnet

el faro
el faroh
headlight

MEGANE

el neumático
el ne-oomateekoh
tyre

el motor
el motor
engine

el parachoques
el parachokais
bumper

THE CONTROLS

el airbag
el ahyeerbag
airbag

las luces de emergencia
lahs loothais day aimerhenthya
hazard lights

el salpicadero
el salpeekaderoh
dashboard

el volante
el bolantay
steering wheel

el velocímetro
el belotheemetroh
speedometer

el cláxon
el klakson
horn

el equipo estéreo del coche
el ekeepoh estereoh dail kochay
car stereo

la palanca de cambios
lah palankah day kambyos
gear stick

la calefacción
lah kalefakthyon
heater

ROAD SIGNS

sentido obligatorio
senteedo ohbleegatoryoh
one way

glorieta
gloryetah
roundabout

ceda el paso
thedah el pasoh
give way

calzada con prioridad
kalthadah kon pryoreedad
priority road

entrada prohibida
entradah proybeedah
no entry

estacionamiento prohibido
estathyonamyentoh proybeedoh
no parking

velocidad máxima
belotheedad makseemah
speed limit

peligro
peleegroh
hazard

la autopista
lah ahootopeestah
motorway

la vía de acceso
lah bee-ah day akthesoh
sliproad

ON THE ROAD

el parquímetro
el parkeemetroh
parking meter

el semáforo
el saimaforoh
traffic light

el guardia de tráfico
el gwardyah day trafeekoh
traffic policeman

el mapa
el mapah
map

el teléfono de emergencias
el telefonoh day aimerhenthyas
emergency phone

el paso de peatones
el pahsoh day peahtonais
pedestrian crossing

el atasco
el ahtaskoh
traffic jam

el aparcamiento para minusválidos
el ahparkamyentoh parah meenoosbaleedos
disabled parking

AT THE STATION

Where can I buy a ticket?	¿Dónde se puede comprar un billete? *donday say pweday komprar oon beeyetay*
Is there an automatic ticket machine?	¿Hay una máquina de billetes? *ah-ee oonah makeenah day beeyetais*

la máquina expendedora de billetes
lah makeenah ekspendedorah day beeyetais
automatic ticket machine

How much is a ticket to…?	¿Cuánto cuesta un billete para…? *kwantoh kwestah oon beeyetay parah*
Two tickets to…	Dos billetes para… *dos beeyetais parah*
I'd like…	Quisiera… *keesyerah*
…a single ticket to…	…un billete de ida para… *oon beeyetay day eedah parah*
…a return ticket to…	…un billete de ida y vuelta para… *oon beeyetay day eedah ee bweltah parah*
…a first class ticket	…un billete de clase preferente *oon beeyetay day klasay praiferentay*
…a standard class ticket	…un billete de clase turista *oon beeyetay day klasay tooreestah*

I'd like to…	Quisiera… *keesyerah*
…reserve a seat	…reservar un asiento *reserbar oon uhsyentoh*
…AVE/TALGO…	…en el AVE/TALGO para… *en el ahbay/talgoh parah*
…book a couchette	…reservar una litera *reserbar oonah leeterah*
Is there a reduction…?	¿Hay descuentos… *ah-ee daiskwentos*
…for children?	…para niños? *parah neenyos*
…for students?	…para estudiantes? *parah estoodyantais*
…for senior citizens?	…para la tercera edad? *parah lah tertherah edad*
Is there a restaurant car?	¿Hay vagón restaurante? *ah-ee bagon raista-oorantuy*
Is it a high-speed train?	¿Es un tren de alta velocidad? *es oon tren day altah belotheedad*
Is it a fast/slow train?	¿Es un tren rápido/lento? *es oon tren rapeedoh/ lentoh*

You may hear…

- **El tren sale de la vía número…**
  el tren salay day lah beeyah noomeroh
  The train leaves from platform…

- **Deberá hacer trasbordo en…**
  deberah ahthair trasbordoh
  You must change trains at…

TRAVELLING BY TRAIN

Do you have a timetable?	¿Tiene un horario? *Tyenay oon ohraryoh*
What time is...	¿A qué hora sale... *ah kay ohrah salay*
...the next train to...?	...el próximo tren para...? *el prokseemoh tren parah*
...the last train to...?	...el último tren para...? *el oolteemoh tren parah*
Which platform does it leave from?	¿De qué vía sale? *day kay beeyah salay*
What time does it arrive in...?	¿A qué hora llega a...? *ah kay ohrah yegah ah*
How long does it take?	¿Cuánto tarda? *kwantoh tardah*
Is this the train for...?	¿Es éste el tren para...? *es estay el tren parah*
Is this the right platform for...?	¿Es ésta la vía del tren para...? *es estah lah beeyah dayl tren parah*
Where is platform three?	¿Dónde está la vía tres? *donday estah lah beeyah trais*
Does this train stop at...?	¿Este tren para en...? *estay tren parah en*

You may hear...

- ¿Ha comprado el billete por Internet?
  ah kompradoh el beeyetay por internet
  Did you book on the Internet?

- Tiene que imprimirlo en la máquina.
  tyenay kay eempreemeerloh en lah makeenah
  Go to the collection point.

Where do I change for...?	¿Dónde tengo que hacer trasbordo para...? *donday taingoh kay ahthair trasbordoh parah*
Is this seat free?	¿Está ocupado este asiento? *estah okoopadoh estay ahsyentoh*
I've reserved this seat	Tengo reservado este asiento *taingoh reserbadoh estay ahsyentoh*
Do I get off here?	¿Tengo que bajarme aquí? *taingoh kay baharmay ahkee*
Where is the underground station?	¿Dónde está la boca de metro? *donday estah lah bokah day metroh*
Which line goes to...?	¿Qué línea va a...? *kay leenay-ah bah ah*

la sala de la estación
lah salah day lah estathyon
concourse

el tren
el tren
train

el vagón comedor
el bagon komedor
dining car

la litera
lah leeterah
couchette

BUSES

When is the next bus to…?	¿Cuándo sale el próximo autobús para…? *kwandoh salay el prokseemoh ah-ootoboos parah*
What is the fare to…?	¿Cuál es la tarifa para…? *kwal es lah tareefah parah*
Where is the nearest bus stop?	¿Dónde está la parada más próxima? *donday estah lah paradah mas prokseemah*
Is this the bus stop for…	¿Es ésta la parada de…? *es estah las paradah day*
Does the number 4 stop here?	¿Para aquí el autobús número 4? *parah ahkee el ah-ootoboos noomeroh kwatroh*
Where can I buy a ticket?	¿Dónde se puede comprar un billete? *donday say pweday komprar oon beeyetay*
Can I pay on the bus?	¿Se puede pagar en el autobús? *say pweday pagar en el ah-ootoboos*
Which buses go to the city centre?	¿Qué autobuses van al centro? *kay ah-ootoboosays ban al thentroh*
I want to get off!	¡Quiero apearme! *kyeroh ahpai-armay*

la estación de autobuses
lah estathyon day ah-ootoboosays
bus station

TAXIS

Where can I get a taxi?	¿Dónde se puede coger un taxi? *donday say pweday kohair oon taksi*
Can I order a taxi?	¿Puedo pedir un taxi? *pwedoh paideer oon taksi*
I want a taxi to…	Quisiera un taxi para ir a… *keesyerah oon taksi parah eer ah*
Can you take me to…	Lléveme a… *yebemeh ah*
Is it far?	¿Está lejos? *estah lehos*
How much will it cost?	¿Cuánto cuesta? *kwantoh kwestah*
Can you drop me here?	¿Puede parar aquí? *pweday parar ahkee*
What do I owe you?	¿Cuánto le debo? *kwantoh lay deboh*
I don't have any change	¿Tiene cambio? *tyenay kambyo*
Keep the change	Quédese con el cambio *kedesay kon el kambyo*
Please can I have a receipt	¿Puede darme un recibo? *pweday darmay oon retheeboh*
Please wait for me	Espéreme, por favor *esperemay por fabor*

el taxi
el taksi
taxi

BOATS

Are there any boat trips?	¿Hay excursiones en barco? *ah-ee ekskoorsyonais en barkoh*
Where does the boat leave from?	¿De dónde sale el barco? *day donday salay el barkoh*
When is...	¿Cuándo sale... *kwandoh salay*
...the next boat to...?	...el próximo barco para...? *el prokseemoh barkoh parah*
...the first boat?	...el primer barco? *el preemair barkoh*
...the last boat?	...el último barco? *el oolteemoh barkoh*
I'd like two tickets for...	Quisiera dos billetes para... *keesyerah dos beeyetais parah*
...the cruise	...el crucero *el krootheroh*

el ferry
el ferry
ferry

el aliscafo
el ahleeskafoh
hydrofoil

el yate
el yatay
yacht

el aerodeslizador
el ahairodesleethador
hovercraft

...the river trip	...la excursión por el río *lah ekskoorsyon por el reeo*
How much is it for...	¿Cuánto cuesta... *kwantoh kwestah*
...a car and two people?	...un coche y dos personas? *oon kochay ee dos personas*
...a family?	...una familia? *oonah fameelya*
...a cabin	...un camarote *oon kahmahrohtay*
Can I buy a ticket on board?	¿Se puede comprar el billete a bordo? *say pweday komprar el beeyetay ah bordoh*
Is there wheelchair access?	¿Dispone de acceso para sillas de ruedas? *deesponay day akthaisoh parah seeyas day rwedas*

el chaleco salvavidas
el chalekoh salbabeedas
lite jacket

el salvavidas
el salbabeedas
lifebuoy

el catamarán
el katamaran
catamaran

el barco de recreo
el barkoh day raikreoh
pleasure boat

AIR TRAVEL

Which terminal do I need?	¿A qué terminal tengo que ir? *ah kay termeenal taingoh kay eer*
Where do I check in?	¿Dónde hay que facturar? *donday ah-y kay faktoorar*
Where is...	¿Dónde está... *donday estah*
...the arrivals hall?	...el vestíbulo de llegadas? *el besteebooloh day yegadas*
...the departures hall?	...el vestíbulo de salidas? *el besteebooloh day saleedas*
...the boarding gate?	...la puerta de embarque? *lah pwertah day embarkay*
I'm travelling...	Viajo en... *beeyahoh en*
...economy	...clase turista *klasay tooreestah*
...business class	...clase preferente *klasay praiferentay*

la bolsa de viaje
lah bolsah day beeyahay
holdall

la comida de avión
lah komeedah day ahbyon
flight meal

el pasaporte
el pasaportay
passport

la tarjeta de embarque
lah tarhetah day embarkay
boarding pass

I'm checking in one suitcase	Facturo una maleta *faktooroh oonah maletch*
I packed it myself	Yo mismo he hecho la maleta *yoh meesmoh eh echoh lah maletah*
I have one piece of hand luggage	Llevo equipaje de mano *yeboh ekeepahay day manoh*
How much is excess baggage?	¿Cuánto hay que pagar por exceso de equipaje? *kwantoh ah-ee kay pagar por eksthesoh day ekeepahay*
Will a meal be served?	¿Se servirá alguna comida? *se serbeerah algoonah komeedah*
I'd like...	Quisiera... *keesyerah*
...a window seat	...un asiento de ventanilla *oon asyentoh day bentaneeyah*
...an aisle seat	...un asiento de pasillo *oon asyentoh day paseeyoh*
...a bulk head seat	...un asiento de mamparo *oon asyentoh day mamparoh*

You may hear...

- Su pasaporte/billete, por favor.
  soo pasaportay/beeyetay por fabor
  Your passport/ticket, please.

- ¿Es éste su bolso?
  es estay soo bolsoh
  Is this your bag?

AT THE AIRPORT

Here's my…	Aquí tiene… *ahkee tyenay*
…boarding pass	…mi tarjeta de embarque *mee tarhetah day embarkay*
…passport	…mi pasaporte *mee pasaportay*
Can I change some money?	¿Puedo cambiar dinero? *pwedoh kambyar deeneroh*

los cheques de viaje
los chekais day beeyahay
traveller's cheque

el control de pasaportes
el kontrol day pasaportais
passport control

What is the exchange rate?	¿A cuánto está el cambio? *ah kwantoh estah el kambyo*
Is the flight delayed?	¿El vuelo llega con retraso? *el bweloh yegah kon raitrasoh*
How late is it?	¿Tiene mucho retraso? *tyenay moochoh raitrasoh*
Which gate does flight… leave from?	¿De qué puerta sale el vuelo…? *day kay pwertah salay el bweloh*
What time do I board?	¿A qué hora tengo que embarcar? *ah kay ohrah taingoh kay embarkar*
When does the gate close?	¿Cuándo cierra la puerta de embarque? *kwandoh thyerah lah pwertah day embarkay*

Where are the trolleys?	¿Dónde están los carritos? *donday estan los karreetos*
Here is the reclaim tag	Ésta es la etiqueta de identificación de equipaje *estah es lah eteeketah day eedenteefeekathyon day ekeepahay*
I can't find my baggage	No encuentro mi equipaje *noh enkwentroh mee ekeepahay*

la tienda libre de impuestos
lah tyendah leebray day eempwestos
duty-free shop

la azafata
lah athafatah
air stewardess

el avión
el ahbyon
aeroplane

la recogida de equipajes
lah rekoheedah day ekeepahais
baggage reclaim

EATING OUT

It is not difficult to eat well and inexpensively in Spain. You can choose from cafés and bars, which serve a range of drinks and hot and cold snacks (*tapas*), as well as family-run restaurants, offering regional dishes, and more formal establishments. After a light breakfast, the Spanish tend to eat a substantial lunch between 2pm and 3pm followed by a *siesta*, and most do not eat their evening meal until after 10pm – very late by our standards.

MAKING A RESERVATION

I'd like to book a table...	Quisiera reservar una mesa... *keesyerah reserbar oonah mesah*
...for lunch/dinner	...para comer/cenar *parah komair/thenar*
...for four people	...para cuatro personas *parah kwatroh personas*
...for this evening	...para esta noche *parah estah nochay*
...for tomorrow at one	...para mañana a la una *parah manyanah ah lah oonah*
...for lunchtime today	...para hoy al mediodía *parah oi al medyodeeya*
Do you have a table earlier/later?	¿Tiene una mesa más temprano/tarde? *tyenay oonah mesah mas taimpranoh/tarday*
My name is...	Me llamo... *may yamoh*
My telephone number is...	Mi número de teléfono es... *mee noomeroh day telefonoh es*
I have a reservation	Tengo una reserva *taingoh oonah reserbah*
in the name of...	a nombre de... *ah nombray day*
We haven't booked	No tenemos reserva *noh tainemos reserbah*
Can we sit here?	¿Podemos sentarnos aquí? *podemos saintarnos ahkee*
We'd like a table near the window	Quisiéramos una mesa cerca de la ventana *keesyeramos oonah mesah therkah day lah bentanah*
We'd like to eat outside	Quisiéramos comer fuera *keesyeramos komair fwerah*

ORDERING A MEAL

Can we see the menu?	¿Nos trae la carta?
	nos tra-ay lah kartah
...the wine list?	...la carta de vinos?
	lah kartah day beenos
Do you have...	¿Tienen...
	tyenain
...a set menu?	...un menú del día?
	oon menoo dail deeyah
...a fixed-price menu?	...un menú a precio fijo?
	oon menoo ah prethyo feehoh
...a children's menu?	...un menú para niños?
	oon menoo parah neenyos
...an à la carte menu	...un menú a la carta?
	oon menoo ah lah kartah
What are today's specials?	¿Cuál es el plato del día?
	kwal es el plahto del deeyah
What are the local specialities?	¿Cuáles son los platos típicos?
	kwales son los plahtos teepeekos
What do you recommend?	¿Qué recomienda?
	kay raikomyendah

You may hear...

- **¿Tiene una reserva?**
  tyenay oonah reserbah
  Do you have a reservation?

- **¿A nombre de quién?**
  ah nombray day kyen
  In what name?

- **Tomen asiento.**
  tomain ahsyentoh
  Please be seated.

- **¿Están listos para pedir?**
  estan leestos parah paideer
  Are you ready to order?

What is this?	¿Qué es esto? *kay es estoh*
Are there any vegetarian dishes?	¿Hay platos vegetarianos? *ah-ee plahtos behetar-anos*
I can't eat…	No puedo comer… *noh pwedoh komair*
…dairy foods	…productos lácteos *prodooktos laktai-os*
…nuts	…frutos secos *frootos sekos*
…wheat	…trigo *treegoh*
To drink, I'll have…	Para beber, tomaré… *parah bebair tomaray*
Can we have…	¿Nos trae… *nos tra-ay*
…some water	…agua? *awa*
…some bread?	…pan? *pan*
…the dessert menu?	…la carta de postres? *lch kartah day postrais*

Reading the menu

• **Entrantes** *entrantais*	Starters
• **Primeros platos** *preemeros plahtos*	First courses
• **Segundos platos** *saigoondos plahtos*	Main courses
• **Verduras** *berdooras*	Vegetables
• **Quesos** *kaisos*	Cheeses
• **Postres** *postrais*	Desserts

COMPLAINING

I didn't order this	Esto no es lo que he pedido *estoh noh es loh kay eh paideedoh*
When is our food coming?	¿Cuándo nos servirán la comida? *kwandoh nos serbeeran lah komeedah*
We can't wait any longer	No podemos esperar más *noh podemos esperar mas*

PAYING

The bill, please	La cuenta, por favor *lah kwentah por fabor*
Can we pay separately?	¿Podemos pagar por separado? *podemos pagar por saiparadoh*
Can I have...	¿Me da... *may dah*
...a receipt?	...un comprobante? *oon komprobantay*
...an itemized bill?	...una cuenta desglosada? *oonah kwentah daisglosadah*
Is service included?	¿Está incluido el servicio? *Estah eenklooydoh el serbeethyo*

You may hear...

- **No aceptamos tarjetas de crédito.**
  noh ahtheptamos tarhetas day kredeetoh
  We don't take credit cards.

- **Por favor, introduzca su pin.**
  por fabor eentrodoothkah soo peen
  Please enter your PIN.

CROCKERY AND CUTLERY

el plato de postre
el plahtoh day postray
side plate

el cuenco
el kwenkoh
bowl

la sal
lah sal
salt

la pimienta
lah peemyentah
pepper

la taza y el plato
lah tahthah y el plahtoh
cup and saucer

la cucharilla de café
lah koochareeyah day kafay
teaspoon

la copa
lah kopah
glass

la cuchara de postre
lah koocharah day postray
dessertspoon

el cuchillo
el koocheeyoh
knife

la servilleta
lah serbeeyetah
napkin

el tenedor
el tainedor
fork

el plato llano
el plahtoh yanoh
dinner plate

AT THE CAFÉ OR BAR

The menu, please	La carta, por favor *lah kartah por fabor*
Do you have…?	¿Tienen…? *tyenain*
What fruit juices/herb teas do you have?	¿Qué zumos de frutas/ infusiones tienen? *kay thoomos day frootas/ eenfoosyonais tyenain*
I'd like…	Quisiera… *keesyerah*
I'll have…	Tomaré… *tomaray*

un café con leche
oon kafay kon lechay
white coffee

un café solo
oon kafay soloh
black coffee

un cortado
oon kortadoh
black coffee with dash of milk

un chocolate a la taza
oon chokolatay ah lah tathah
hot chocolate

You may hear...

- ¿Qué van a tomar?
  kay ban ah tomar
  What would you like?

- ¿Algo más?
  algoh mas
  Anything else?

- De nada.
  day nadah
  You're welcome.

un té con leche
oon tay kon lechay
tea with milk

un té con limón
oon tay kon leemon
tea with lemon

un poleo
oon polech
mint tea

un té verde
oon tay berday
green tea

una manzanilla
oonah manthaneeyah
camomile tea

una horchata
oonah orchatah
tiger nut milk

A bottle of…	Una botella de… *oonah botaiyah day*
A glass of…	Un vaso de/una copa de… *oon basoh day/oonah kopah day*
A cup of…	Una taza de… *oonah tathah day*
With lemon/milk	con limón/leche *kon leemon/lechay*
Another…please	Otro…por favor *otroh…por fabor*
The same again, please	Lo mismo, por favor *loh meesmoh por fabor*

CAFÉ AND BAR DRINKS

un café helado
oon kafay ehladoh
iced coffee

un zumo de naranja
oon thoomoh day naranhah
fresh orange juice

un zumo de manzana
oon thoomoh day manthanah
apple juice

un zumo de piña
oon thoomoh day peenyah
pineapple juice

un zumo de tomate
oon thoomoh day tomatay
tomato juice

un mosto
oon mostoh
grape juice

una limonada
oonah leemonadah
lemonade

una naranjada
oonah naranhadah
orangeade

una cola
oonah kolah
cola

agua mineral
awa meeneral
mineral water

una cerveza
oonah thairbaithah
beer

un tinto con gaseosa
oon teentoh kon gasecsah
red wine and lemonade

un vino tinto
oon beenoh teentoh
red wine

el vino blanco
el beenoh blankoh
white wine

una copa de jerez
oonah kopah day hairaith
glass of sherry

una jarra de sangría
oonah harrah day sangrʌa
jug of sangria

You may hear...

- ¿Una caña?
  oonah kanyah
  A half?

- ¿En botella o de barril?
  en botaiyah oh day barreel
  Bottled or draught?

- ¿Con gas o sin gas?
  kon gas oh seen gas
  Still or sparkling?

- ¿Con hielo?
  kon yeloh
  With ice?

BAR SNACKS

el bocadillo
el bokadeeyoh
sandwich

los frutos secos
los frootos saikos
nuts

las aceitunas
las ahthaytoonas
olives

la ensalada
lah ensaladah
salad

el aliño
el ahleenyoh
dressing

las empanadillas
las empanadeeyas
pastry

las tapas (albóndigas)
las tapas (albondeegas)
tapas (meatballs)

el chorizo
el choreethoh
chorizo

la tortilla
lah torteeyah
omelette

el helado
el ehladoh
ice cream

FAST FOOD

Can I have…	¿Me da… _may dah_
…to eat in/take away	…para comer aquí/ para llevar? _parah komair ahkee/ parah yebar_
…some ketchup/mustard	…ketchup/mostaza _ketchoop/mostatah_

la hamburguesa
lah amboorgaisah
hamburger

la hamburguesa de pollo
lah amboorgaisah day poyoh
chicken burger

el rollo
el royoh
wrap

el frankfurt
el frankfoort
hot dog

el pinchito
el peencheetoh
kebab

las patatas fritas
las patatas freetas
French fries

el pollo frito
el poyoh freetoh
fried chicken

la pizza
lah peetsah
pizza

BREAKFAST

Can I have…	¿Me trae… *may tra-ay*
…some milk	…leche? *lechay*
…some sugar	…azúcar? *ahthookar*
…some artificial sweetener	…edulcorante artificial? *edoolkorantay arteefeethyal*
…some butter	…mantequilla? *mantaikeeyah*
… some jam?	…confitura? *konfeetoorah*

un café
 oon kafay
 coffee

un té
 oon tay
 tea

un chocolate a la taza
 oon chokolatay ah lah tathah
 hot chocolate

un zumo de naranja
 oon thoomoh day naranhah
 orange juice

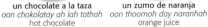

un zumo de manzana
 oon thoomoh day manthanah
 apple juice

el pan
 el pan
 bread

un panecillo
oon panetheeyoh
bread roll

los churros
los choorros
churros

un cruasán
oon crwasan
croissant

una mermelada
oonah mermeladah
marmalade

la miel
la myail
honey

los huevos revueltos
los webos rebweltos
scrambed eggs

un huevo duro
oon weboh dooroh
boiled egg

un huevo escalfado
con weboh eskalfadoh
poached egg

la fruta fresca
lah frootah fraiskah
fresh fruit

un yogurt de frutas
oon yogoort day frootes
fruit yoghurt

FIRST COURSES

la sopa
lah sopah
soup

el caldo
el kaldoh
broth

la sopa de pescado
lah sopah day peskadoh
fish soup

la sopa de ajo
lah sopah day aho
garlic soup

el gazpacho
el gathpachoh
gazpacho

las gambas a la plancha
las gambas ah lah planchah
grilled prawns

los mejillones
los meheeyonais
mussels

el calamar frito
el kalamar freetoh
fried squid

el marisco frito
el mareeskoh freetoh
fried seafood

la ensalada de marisco
lah ensaladah day mareeskoh
seafood salad

el pescado adobado
el peskadoh adobadoh
marinated fish

los huevos rellenos de atún
los webos rayenos day atoon
tuna stuffed eggs

el revuelto de gambas
el raibweltoh day gambas
scrambled egg and prawns

el suflé
el sooflay
soufflé

la tortilla
lah torteeyah
omelette

la tortilla de patatas
lah torteeyah day patatas
Spanish omelette

los tomates rellenos
los tomatais rayenos
stuffed tomato

las berenjenas rellenas
las berenhenas rayenas
stuffed aubergines

el jamón serrano
el hamon sairanoh
cured ham

los entremeses variados
los entraimesais baryados
cold platter

MAIN COURSES

I would like…	Tráigame… *traygamay*
…the chicken	…el pollo *el poyoh*
…the duck	…el pato *el patoh*
…the lamb	…el cordero *el korderoh*
…the pork	…el cerdo *el thairdoh*
…the beef	…la ternera *lah ternerah*
…the steak	…el filete *el feeletay*
…the veal	…la ternera lechal *lah ternerah laichal*
…the liver	…el hígado *el eegadoh*
roast	asado/a *asadoh/ah*
baked	al horno *al ornoh*
grilled	a la plancha *ah lah planchah*
on skewers	en brocheta *en brochaitah*

You may see…

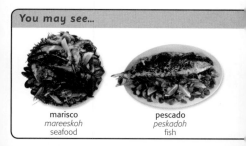

marisco
mareeskoh
seafood

pescado
peskadoh
fish

You may hear...

- **¿Cómo quiere el filete?**
  komoh kyeray el feeletay
  How do you like your steak?

- **¿Poco hecho, bien hecho?**
  pokoh echoh byen echoh
  Rare or medium?

- **¿Muy hecho?**
  mooy echoh
  Well done?

barbecued	a la parrilla *ah lah parreeyah*
poached	cocido a fuego lento *kotheedoh ah fwegoh lentoh*
boiled	hervido/a *erbeedoh/ah*
fried	frito/a *freetoh/ah*
pan-fried/sautéed	frito/salteado *freeetoh/saltai-ah doh*
stuffed	relleno/a *rayenoh/ah*
stewed	estofado/a *aistofadoh/ah*
with cheese	con queso *kon kaisoh*

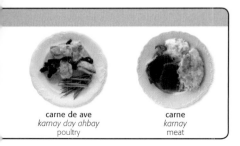

carne de ave
karnay day ahbay
poultry

carne
karnay
meat

SALADS AND SIDE DISHES

las patatas fritas
las patatas freetas
fried potatoes

la menestra de verduras
lah menestrah day berdooras
mixed vegetables

la ensalada de lechuga
lah ensaladah day laichoogah
green salad

la ensalada mixta
lah ensaladah meekstah
mixed salad

la ensalada de pan
lah ensaladah day pan
bread salad

el arroz
el ahrroth
rice

el arroz con verduras
el ahrroth kon berdooras
rice with vegetables

la berenjena rellena
lah berenhena rayenah
stuffed aubergine

los pimientos rellenos
los peemyentos raiyenos
stuffed peppers

las patatas fritas
las patatas freetas
chips

DESSERTS

I would like…	Tráigame… *traygamay*
…with cream	…con nata *kon natah*
…with ice cream	…con helado *kon ehladoh*
…with chocolate sauce	…con chocolate deshecho *kon chocolatay daisechoh*

la mousse de chocolate
lah moos day chokolatay
chocolate mousse

la crema catalana
lah kraimah katalanah
egg custard

las natillas
las nateeyas
custard pudding

el flan
el flan
crème caramel

el sorbete
el sorbetay
sorbet

el helado
el ehladoh
ice cream

el pastel
el pastail
cake

la tarta de frutas
lah tarta day frootas
fruit tart

PLACES TO STAY

Spain has a wide range of places to stay, depending on your personal preference and budget. These range from historic *paradores* and luxurious hotels to smaller, family-run *pensiones* (guest houses) and basic *hostales*. If you want a self-catering option, however, you can rent a seaside villa or city apartment or find a campsite to park your caravan or put up your tent.

MAKING A RESERVATION

I'd like…	Quisiera… *keesyerah*
…to make a reservation	…hacer una reserva *ahthair oonah reserbah*
…a double room	…una habitación doble *oonah ahbeetathyon dohblay*
…a twin-bedded room	…una habitación con dos camas *oonah ahbeetathyon kon dos kamas*
…a single room	…una habitación individual *oonah ahbeetathyon eendeebeedwal*
…a family room	…una habitación familiar *oonah ahbeetathyon fameelyar*
…with a bath/shower	…con baño/ducha *kon banyoh/doochah*
…with a sea view	…con vistas al mar *kon beestas al mar*
…with a balcony	…con balcón *kon balkon*
…for two nights	…para dos noches *parah dos nochais*
…for a week	…para una semana *parah oonah semanah*
Is breakfast included?	¿El desayuno está incluido en el precio? *el daisayoonoh estah eenclooydoh en el prethyo*
How much is it…	¿Cuánto cuesta… *kwanto kwestah*
…per night?	…por noche? *por nochay*
…per week?	…por semana? *por semanah*

CHECKING IN

I have a reservation.	Tengo una reserva. *taingoh oonah reserbah*
Do you have…	¿Hay… *ah-ee*

un botones
oon botonais
a porter

ascensores
asthensorais
lifts

servicio de habitaciones
serbeethyo day ahbeetathyones
room service

el minibar
el meeneebar
mini bar

I'd like…	Quisiera… *keesyerah*
…the keys for room…	…la llave de la habitación… *lah yabay day lah ahbeetathyon*
…a wake-up call at…	…que me despierten por la mañana a las… *kay meh despyertan por lah manyanah ah las*
What time is…	¿A qué hora se sirve… *ah kay ohrah say seerbay*
…breakfast?	…el desayuno? *el daisayoonoh*

IN YOUR ROOM

Do you have…	¿Tiene… *tyenay*
another…	otro/a … *ohtroh/ah*
some more…	más… *mas*

las almohadas
las almoadas
pillows

las mantas
las mantas
blankets

una bombilla
oonah bombeeyah
a light bulb

un adaptador
oon ahdaptador
an adapter

I've lost my key

He perdido la llave
eh pairdeedoh la yabay

You may hear…

- El número de su habitación es…
  el noomeroh day soo ahbeetathyon es
  Your room number is…

- Aquí tiene la llave.
  ahkee tyenay lah yabay
  Here is your key.

IN THE HOTEL

The room is…	En la habitación hace… *en lah ahbeetathyon ahthay*
…too hot	…demasiado calor *demasyadoh kalor*
…too cold	…demasiado frío *demasyadoh freeyo*

el termostato
el termostatoh
thermostat

el radiador
el radyador
radiator

la habitación doble
lah ahbeetathyon dohblay
double room

el hervidor de agua
el erbeedor day awa
kettle

The room is too small	La habitación es demasiado pequeña *lah ahbeetathyon es demasyadoh pekenya*
The window won't open	La ventana no se abre *la bentanah noh say abray*
I can't get an outside line	No tengo línea con el exterior *noh taingoh leenayah kon el ekstairyor*
The TV doesn't work	El televisor no funciona *el telebeesor noh foonthyonah*

la percha
lah perchah
coat hanger

el televisor
el telebeesor
television

la persiana de lamas
lah persyanah day lamas
venetian blind

el mando a distancia
el mandoh ah deestanthya
remote control

CHECKING OUT

When do I have to vacate the room?	¿Cuándo hay que dejar la habitación? *kwandoh ah-ee kay dehar lah ahbeetathyon*
Is there a porter to carry my bags?	¿Hay un botones para llevarme las maletas? *ah-ee oon botonais parah yebarmay las maletahs*
Can I have the bill, please.	¿Me da la cuenta, por favor? *meh dah lah kwentah por fabor*
Can I pay by credit card?	¿Puedo pagar con tarjeta de crédito? *pwedoh pagar kon tarhetah day kredeetoh*
I'd like a receipt	¿Podría darme un comprobante? *podrya darmay oon komprobantay*

IN THE BATHROOM

la bañera
lah banyerah
bathtub

el bidé
el beeday
bidet

el jabón
el habon
soap

las toallas
las toah-yas
towels

el albornoz
el albornoth
bathrobe

el baño de burbujas
el banyo day boorboohas
bubblebath

el gel de ducha
el hel day doochah
shower gel

el desodorante
el desodorantay
deodorant

la loción corporal
lah lothyon korporal
body lotion

el dentífrico
el denteefreekoh
toothpaste

el cepillo de dientes
el thepeeyoh day dyentes
toothbrush

el enjuague bucal
el enhwagay bookal
mouthwash

la maquinilla eléctrica
lah makeeneeya elektreekah
electric razor

la espuma de afeitar
lah espoomah day ahfeytar
shaving foam

la maquinilla de afeitar
lah makeeneeya day ahfeytar
razor

el secador de pelo
el sekador day peloh
hairdryer

el champú
el champoo
shampoo

el suavizante
el swabeethantay
conditioner

el cortaúñas
el kortaoonyas
nail clippers

las tijeras para las uñas
las teeheras parah las oonyas
nail scissors

SELF-CATERING

Can we have...	¿Me da... _meh dah_
...the key, please?	...la llave, por favor? _lah yabay por fabor_
...an extra bed?	...una cama extra? _oonah kamah ekstrah_
...a child's bed?	...una camita de niño? _oonah kameetah day neenyoh_

la trona
lah tronah
high chair

la cuna
la kunah
cot

...more cutlery, crockery	...más cubiertos, vajilla _mas koobyertos baheeyah_
Where is...	¿Dónde está... _donday estah_
...the fusebox?	...la caja de los plomos? _lah kahah day los plomos_
...the stopcock?	...la llave de paso? _lah yabay day pasoh_
...the nearest doctor?	...el médico más cercano? _el medeekoh mas therkanoh_
...the nearest shop?	... la tienda más cercana? _la tyendah mas therkanah_
Do you do babysitting?	¿Ofrecen servicio de canguro? _ofrethain serbeethyo day kangooroh_
How does the heating work?	¿Cómo funciona la calefacción? _komoh foonthyonah lah kalefakthyon_

Is there…	¿Hay… *ah-ee*
…air conditioning?	…aire acondicionado? *aheeray ahkondeethyonado*
…central heating?	…calefacción central? *kalefakthyon thentral*
When does the cleaner come?	¿Cuándo vienen a limpiar? *kwandoh byenen ah leempyar*

el ventilador
el benteelador
fan

la estufa eléctrica
lah estoofah elektreekah
convector heater

Where do I put the rubbish?	¿Dónde pongo la basura? *donday pongoh lah basoorah*
Who do we contact if there are problems?	¿A quién llamamos si hay problemas? *ah kyen yamamos see ah-ee problaimas*
Do you take pets?	¿Aceptan animales domésticos? *ahtheptan ahneemales domesteekos*

el perro
el perroh
dog

IN THE VILLA

Is there an inventory?	¿Hay un inventario? *ah-ee oon eenbentaryoh*
Where is this item?	¿Dónde está este objeto? *donday estah estay obhetoh*
I need…	Necesito… *netheseetoh*
…an adapter	…un adaptador *oon ahdaptador*
…an extension lead	…un alargador *oon ahlargador*
…a torch	…una linterna *oonah leenternah*
…matches	…cerillas *thereeyas*

el microondas
el meekro-ondas
microwave

la plancha
lah planchah
iron

la tabla de planchar
lah tablah day planchar
ironing board

la fregona y el cubo
lah fregonah ee el kooboh
mop and bucket

el recogedor y el cepillo
el raikohedor ee el thepeeyoh
dust pan and brush

el detergente
el daiterhentay
detergent

PROBLEM SOLVING

The shower doesn't work	La ducha no funciona *lah doochah noh foonthyona*
The toilet is leaking	El váter tiene un escape *el bater tyenay oon escahpay*
Can you mend it today?	¿Puede arreglarlo hoy? *pweday arreglarloh oy*
There's no...	No hay... *noh ah-ee*
...electricity	...electricidad *elektreetheedad*
...water	...agua *awa*

la lavadora
lah labadorah
washing machine

el frigorífico congelador
el freegoreefeekoh konhelador
fridge-freezer

el cubo de la basura
el kooboh day lah basoorah
rubbish bin

la cerradura y la llave
lah therradoorah ee lah yabay
lock and key

la alarma de incendios
lah alarmah day eenthendyos
smoke alarm

el extintor
el eksteentor
fire extinguisher

KITCHEN EQUIPMENT

el abrelatas
el ahbrelatas
can opener

el abrebotellas
el ahbrebotaiyas
bottle opener

el sacacorchos
el sakakorchos
corkscrew

la tabla de cortar
lah tablah day kortar
chopping board

el cuchillo de cocina
el koocheeyoh day kotheenah
kitchen knife

el pelador
el pailador
peeler

el batidor
el bateedor
whisk

la cuchara de madera
lah koocharah day madairah
wooden spoon

la espátula
lah espatoolah
spatula

el rallador
el rayador
grater

el colador
el kolador
colander

la sartén
lah sartain
frying pan

la cacerola
lah katherolah
saucepan

la plancha
lah planchah
grill pan

la olla
lah ohyah
casserole dish

el bol
el bohl
mixing bowl

la licuadora
lah leekwadorah
blender

la bandeja de horno
lah bandeha day ohrnoh
baking tray

las manoplas para el horno
las manoplas parah el ohrnoh
oven gloves

el delantal
el dailantal
apron

CAMPING

Where is the nearest...	¿Dónde está el... *donday estah el*
...campsite?	...camping más cercano? *kampeeng mas therkanoh*
...caravan site?	...camping para caravanas más cercano? *kampeeng parah karabanas mas therkanoh*
Can we camp here?	¿Podemos acampar aquí? *podemos ahkampar ahkee*
Do you have any vacancies?	¿Tiene parcelas libres? *tyenay parthelas leebrais*
What is the charge...	¿Cuánto cuesta... *kwanto kwestah*
...per night?	...por noche? *por nochay*
...per week?	...por semana? *por semanah*
Does the price include...	¿El precio incluye... *el prethyo eenklooyay*
...electricity?	...la electricidad? *lah elektreetheedad*
...hot water?	...el agua caliente? *el awa kalyentay*
We want to stay for...	Queremos quedarnos... *keremos kedarnos*

la piqueta	la tienda	la cuerda tensora
lah peeketah	*lah tyendah*	*lah kwerdah tensorah*
tent peg	tent	guy rope

Can I rent…	¿Se puede alquilar… _say pweday alkeelar_
…a tent?	…una tienda? _oonah tyendah_
…a barbecue?	…una barbacoa? _oonah barbakoah_
Where are…	¿Dónde están… _donday estan_
…the toilets?	…los aseos? _los ahsaios_
…the dustbins?	…los cubos de la basura? _los kcobos day lah basoorah_
Are there…	¿Hay… _ah-ee_
…showers?	… duchas? _dochas_
…laundry facilities?	…servicios de lavandería? _serbeethyos day labandery3_
Is there…	¿Hay. . _ah-ee_
…a swimming pool?	…piscina? _peestheenah_
…a shop?	…una tienda? _oonah tyendah_

You may hear…

- Está prohibido hacer fuego.
  estah proybeedoh ahthair fwegoh
  Don't light a fire.

- El agua no es potable.
  el awa noh es potablay
  Don't drink the water.

AT THE CAMPSITE

el colchón hinchable
el kolchon eenchablay
air mattress

el saco de dormir
el sakoh day dormeer
sleeping bag

el hervidor de agua para camping
el erbeedor day awa parah kampeeng
camping kettle

el hornillo
el ohrneeyoh
camping stove

el termo
el tairmoh
vacuum flask

la nevera
lah naibairah
coolbox

la barbacoa
lah barbakoah
barbecue

el agua embotellada
el awa emboteyadah
bottled water

el cubo
el kooboh
bucket

el repelente de insectos
el repelentay day eensektos
insect repellent

la crema con filtro solar
lah kremah kon feeltroh sohlar
sunscreen

el mazo
el mahthoñ
mallet

la brújula
lah broohoclah
compass

la linterna
lah leenternah
torch

el ovillo de cordel
el ohbeeyoh day kordel
ball of string

el impermeable
el eempermayablay
waterproofs

la tirita
lah teereetah
plaster

las botas para caminar
las botas parah kameenar
walking boots

la mochila
lah mocheelah
backpack

SHOPPING

As well as department stores, supermarkets and specialist shops, Spain has many picturesque open-air markets, held in town squares and high streets, where you can buy fruit, vegetables and regional specialities. Most shops close between 2pm and 5pm for the *siesta* but they do stay open quite late in the evenings. However, many small stores and food shops shut on Saturday afternoons, and few stores open on Sundays.

IN THE STORE

I'm looking for…	Estoy buscando… *estoy booskandoh*
Do you have…?	¿Tiene…? *tyenay*
I'm just looking	Sólo estoy mirando *soloh estoy meerandoh*
I'm being served	Ya me atienden *yah may ahtyendain*
Do you have any more of these?	¿Tiene otros más como éste? *tyenay ohtros mas komoh estay*
How much is this?	¿Cuánto vale esto? *kwantoh balay estoh*
Have you anything cheaper?	¿Tiene otro más barato? *tyenay ohtroh mas baratoh*
I'll take this one	Me llevo éste *may yeboh estay*
Where can I pay?	¿Dónde hay que pagar? *donday ah-ee kay pagar*
I'll pay…	Pagaré… *Pagaray*
…in cash	…en efectivo *en efekteeboh*
…by credit card	…con tarjeta de crédito *kon tarheta day kredeetoh*
Can I have a receipt?	¿Me da un comprobante? *may dah oon komprobantay*
I'd like to exchange this	Quisiera descambiar esto *keesyerah deskambyar estoh*

IN THE BANK

I'd like…	Quisiera… *keesyerah*
…to make a withdrawal	…sacar dinero *sakar deeneroh*
…to pay in some money	…ingresar dinero *eengresar deeneroh*
…to change some money	…cambiar dinero *kambyar deeneroh*
…into euros	…en euros *en eh-ooros*
…into sterling	…en libras *en leebras*
Here is my passport	Tenga mi pasaporte *tengah mee pasaporteh*
My name is…	Me llamo… *may yamoh*
My account number is…	El número de mi cuenta es… *el noomeroh day mee kwentah es*
My bank details are…	Mis datos bancarios son… *mees dahtos bankaryos son*

el tipo de cambio
el teepoh day kambyoh
exchange rate

los cheques de viaje
los chekais day beeyahay
traveller's cheque

el pasaporte
el pasaportay
passport

el dinero
el deeneroh
money

Do I have to...	¿Tengo que... *taingch kay*
...key in my PIN?	...introducir mi pin? *eentrodootheer mee peen*
...sign here?	...firmar aquí? *feermar ahkee*
Is there a cash machine?	¿Hay un cajero automático? *ah-ee oon kaheroh ah-ootomateekoh*
Can I withdraw money on my credit card?	¿Puedo sacar dinero a cuenta de mi tarjeta de crédito? *pwedoh sakar deeneroh ah kwentah day mee tarhetah day kredeetoh*
Can I cash a cheque?	¿Puedo cobrar un cheque? *pwedoh kobrar oon chekay*
When does the bank open/close?	¿Cuándo abre/cierra el banco? *kwandoh ahbray/thyerrah el bankoh*

el cajero automático
el kaheroh ah-ootomateekoh
cash machine

el director del banco
el deerektor dail bankoh
bank manager

la tarjeta de crédito
lah tarhetah day kredeetoh
credit card

el talonario de cheques
el talonaryo day chekais
chequebook

SHOPS

la panadería
lah panaderya
baker's

la verdulería
lah berdoolerya
greengrocer's

la charcutería
lah charkooterya
delicatessen

la pescadería
lah peskaderya
fishmonger

el estanco
el estankoh
tobacconist

la boutique
lah bootik
boutique

la tienda de discos
lah tyendah day deeskos
record shop

la tienda de muebles
lah tyendah day mweblais
furniture shop

la carnicería
lah karneetherya
butcher's

el colmado
el kolmadoh
grocer's

el supermercado
el soopermerkadoh
supermarket

la librería
lah leebrerya
book shop

la zapatería
lah thapaterya
shoe shop

la sastrería
lah sastrerya
tailor's

la joyería
lah hoyairya
jeweller's

la ferretería
lah ferreterya
hardware shop

AT THE MARKET

I would like…	Quisiera… *keesyerah*
How much is this?	¿Cuánto es? *kwantoh es*
What's the price per kilo?	¿A cuánto va el kilo? *ah kwantoh bah el keeloh*
It's too expensive	Es muy caro *es mooy karoh*
Do you have anything cheaper?	¿Tiene algo más barato? *tyenay algoh mas baratoh*
That's fine, I'll take it	Está bien, me lo llevo *estah byen may loh yeboh*
I'll take two kilos	Póngame dos kilos *pongamay dos keelos*
A kilo of…	Un kilo de… *oon keeloh day*
Half a kilo of…	Medio kilo de… *medyo keeloh day*
A little more, please	Un poco más, por favor *oon pokoh mas por fabor*
That's very good. I'll take some	Está muy bueno. Póngame un poco *estah mooy bwenoh pongameh oon pokoh*
That will be all, thank you	Nada más, gracias *nadah mas grathyas*

You may hear...

- ¿Qué desea? *kay daiseah* Can I help you?

- ¿Cuánto le pongo? *kwantoh lay pongoh* How much would you like?

IN THE SUPERMARKET

Where is/are…	¿Dónde está/están… *donday estah/estan*
…the drinks aisle?	…el pasillo de las bebidas? *el paseeyoh day las bebeedas*
…the check-out?	…las cajas? *las kahas*

el carrito
el karreetoh
trolley

la cesta
iah thestah
basket

I'm looking for…	Estoy buscando… *estoy booskandoh*
Do you have any more?	¿Tiene más? *tyenay mas*
Is this reduced?	¿Está rebajado? *estah rebahadoh*
What is the sell-by date?	¿Qué fecha de caducidad tiene? *kay fechah day kadootheedad tyenay*
Where do I pay?	¿Dónde hay que pagar? *donday ah-ee kay pagar*
Shall I key in my PIN?	¿Introduzco el pin? *eentrodoothkoh el peen*
Can I have a bag?	¿Me da una bolsa? *may day oonah bolsah*
Can you help me pack	¿Puede ayudarme a guardar en las bolsas? *pweday ahyoodarmay ah gwardar en las bolsas*

FRUIT

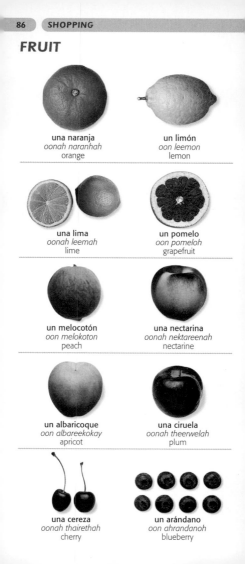

una naranja
oonah naranhah
orange

un limón
oon leemon
lemon

una lima
oonah leemah
lime

un pomelo
oon pomeloh
grapefruit

un melocotón
oon melokoton
peach

una nectarina
oonah nektareenah
nectarine

un albaricoque
oon albareekokay
apricot

una ciruela
oonah theerwelah
plum

una cereza
oonah thairethah
cherry

un arándano
oon ahrandanoh
blueberry

una fresa
oonah fresah
strawberry

una frambuesa
oonah frambwesah
raspberry

un melón
oon mailon
melon

las uvas
las oobas
grapes

un plátano
oon platanoh
banana

una granada
oonah granadah
pomegranate

una manzana
oonah manthanah
apple

una pera
oonah pairah
pear

una piña
oonah peenyah
pineapple

un mango
oon mangoh
mango

VEGETABLES

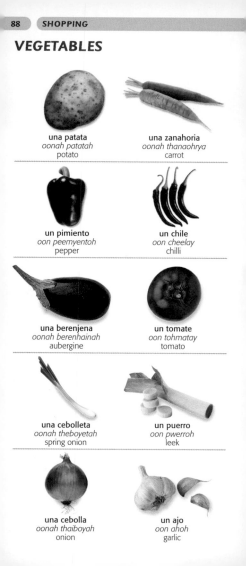

una patata
oonah patatah
potato

una zanahoria
oonah thanaohrya
carrot

un pimiento
oon peemyentoh
pepper

un chile
oon cheelay
chilli

una berenjena
oonah berenhainah
aubergine

un tomate
oon tohmatay
tomato

una cebolleta
oonah theboyetah
spring onion

un puerro
oon pwerroh
leek

una cebolla
oonah thaiboyah
onion

un ajo
oon ahoh
garlic

un champiñón
oon champeenyon
mushroom

un calabacín
oon kalabatheen
courgette

un pepino
oon pepeenoh
cucumber

una judía verde
oonah hoodeeah berday
French bean

el guisante
el gheesantoy
garden peas

un apio
oon ahpeeoh
celery

una espinaca
oonah espeenakah
spinach

un brécol
oon brekol
broccoli

una col
oonah kol
cabbage

una lechuga
ocnah lechoogah
lettuce

MEAT AND POULTRY

May I have…	¿Me pone…
	may pohnay
…a slice of…?	…una loncha de…?
	oonah lonchah day
…a piece of…?	…un trozo de…?
	oon trothoh day

el jamón
el hamon
ham

las salchichas
las salcheechas
sausages

el chorizo
el choreethoh
chorizo

la carne picada
lah karnay peekadah
mince

el filete
el feeletay
steak

el cordero
el korderoh
lamb

el pollo
el poyoh
chicken

el pato
el patoh
duck

FISH AND SHELLFISH

el atún
el ahtoon
tuna

el bacalao
el bakalaoh
cod

la lubina
lah loobeenah
sea bass

el pargo
el pargoh
sea bream

la sardina
lah sardeenah
sardine

el calamar
el kalamar
squid

el pulpo
el poolpoh
octopus

el cangrejo
el kangrehoh
crab

la langosta
lah langostah
lobster

la gamba
lah gambah
prawn

BREAD AND CAKES

el pan blanco
el pan blankoh
white bread

la tortilla
lah torteeyah
tortilla

el cruasán
el crwasan
croissant

el panecillo
el panetheeyoh
roll

las galletas
las gayetas
biscuits

la ensaimada
lah ensaymadah
spiral bun

el trozo de pastel
el trothoh day pastail
slice of cake

la tartaleta de frutas
lah tartaletah day frootas
fruit tart

la madalena
lah madalenah
sponge cake

el pastel de chocolate
el pastail day chocolatay
chocolate cake

DAIRY PRODUCE

la leche entera
lah lechay enterah
whole milk

la leche semidesnatada
lah lechay semeedesnatadah
semi-skimmed milk

la nata
lah natah
cream

el yogurt
el yogoort
yoghurt

la mantequilla
lah mantaikeeyah
butter

el queso seco
el kaisoh saikoh
hard cheese

el queso rallado
el kaisoh rayadoh
grated cheese

el queso de cabra
el kaisoh day kabrah
goat's cheese

el cabrales
el kabralais
Cabrales

el manchego
el manchaigoh
Manchego

NEWSPAPERS AND MAGAZINES

Do you have…	¿Tiene… *tyenay*
…a book of stamps?	…sellos? *seyos*
…airmail stamps?	…sellos de correo por avión? *seyos day korreoh por abhyon*
…a packet of envelopes?	…un paquete de sobres? *oon paketay day sobrais*
…some sticky tape?	…cinta adhesiva? *theentah adeseebah*

una postal
oonah postal
postcard

unos sellos
oonos sayos
stamps

un lápiz
oon lapeeth
pencil

un bolígrafo
oon boleegrafoh
pen

You may hear…

- ¿Cuántos años tiene?
  kwantos ahnyos tyenay
  How old are you?

- ¿Tiene un documento de identidad?
  tyenay oon dokoomentoh day eedenteedad
  Do you have ID?

TABACOS

I'd like...	Quisiera... *keesyerah*
...a pack of cigarettes	...un paquete de tabaco *oon paketay day tabakoh*
...a box of matches	...una caja de cerillas *oonah kahah day thereeyas*

tabaco de liar
tabakoh day lee-ar
tobacco

un mechero
oon mecheroh
lighter

un chicle
oon cheeclay
chewing gum

unos caramelos
oonos karamelos
sweets

un periódico
oon peryodeekoh
newspaper

unas revistas
oonas raibeestas
magazines

un tebeo
oon taibeoh
comic

unos lápices de colores
oonos lapeethais day kolorais
colouring pencils

BUYING CLOTHES

I am looking for…	Estoy buscando… *estoy booskandoh*
I am size…	Gasto la talla… *gastoh lah tayah*
Do you have this…	¿Tiene éste… *tyenay estay*
…in my size?	…en mi talla? *en mee tayah*
…in small	…en la talla pequeña? *en lah tayah pekenya*
…in medium?	…en la talla mediana? *en lah tayah medyanah*
…in large?	…en la talla grande? *en lah tayah granday*
…in other colours?	…en otros colores? *en ohtros kolorais*
Can I try this on?	¿Puedo probármelo? *pwedoh probarmailoh*
It's…	Es… *es*
…too big	…muy grande *mooy granday*
…too small	…muy pequeño *mooy pekenyoh*
I need…	Necesito… *netheseetoh*
…a larger size	…una talla más *oonah tayah mas*
…a smaller size	… una talla menos *oonah tayah menos*
I'll take this one, please	Me llevo éste *may yeboh estay*
Is this on sale?	¿Está rebajado? *estah raibahadoh*

BUYING SHOES

I take shoe size…	Calzo el número… *kalthch el noomeroh*
Can I try…	¿Puedo probarme… *pwedoh probarmay*
…this pair?	…este par? *estay par*
…those ones in the window?	…los del escaparate? *los dail aiskaparatay*
These are…	Me quedan… *may kedan*
…too tight	…muy estrechos *mooy estrechos*
…too big	…muy grandes *mooy grandais*
…too small	… muy pequeños *mooy pekenyos*
These are uncomfortable	Son incómodos *son eenkomodos*
Is there a bigger size?	¿Tienen un número más? *tyenain oon noomeroh mas*
Is there a smaller size?	¿Tienen un número menos? *tyenain oon noomeroh menos*

Clothes and shoe sizes guide

Women's clothes sizes

UK	6	8	10	12	14	16	18	20
Europe	34	36	38	40	42	44	46	48
USA	4	6	8	10	12	14	16	18

Men's clothes sizes

UK	36	38	40	42	44	46	48	50
Europe	46	48	50	52	54	56	58	60
USA	36	38	40	42	44	46	48	50

Women's shoes

UK	3	4	5	6	7	8	9
Europe	36	37	38	39	40	42	43
USA	5	6	7	8	9	10	11

CLOTHES AND SHOES

el vestido
el baisteedoh
dress

el vestido de noche
el baisteedoh day nochay
evening dress

la chaqueta
lah chakaitah
jacket

el jersey
el hairsey
jumper

los tejanos
los tehanos
jeans

la falda
lah faldah
skirt

la zapatilla deportiva
lah thapateeyah daiporteebah
trainer

la bota
lah bohtah
boot

el bolso
el bolsoh
handbag

el cinturón
el theentooron
belt

el traje
el trahay
suit

el abrigo
el abreegoh
coat

la camisa
lah kameesah
shirt

la camiseta
lah kameesetah
t-shirt

los pantalones cortos
los pantalonais kortos
shorts

el zapato de tacón
el thapatoh day takon
high-heel shoe

el zapato de cordones
el thapatoh day kordonais
lace-up shoe

la sandalia
lah sandalyah
sandal

la chancla
lah chanclah
flip-flop

los calcetines
los kaltheteenais
socks

AT THE GIFT SHOP

I'd like to buy a gift for...	Quisiera comprar un regalo para... *keesyerah komprar oon regaloh parah*
...my mother/father	...mi madre/padre *mee madray/padray*
...my daughter/son	...mi hija/hijo *mee eehah/eehoh*
...a child	...un niño *oon neenyoh*
...a friend	...un amigo *oon ahmeegoh*
Can you recommend something?	¿Qué me recomienda? *kay may raikomyendah*
Do you have a box for it?	¿Viene con caja? *byenay kon kahah*
Can you gift-wrap it?	¿Podría envolverlo para regalo? *Podryah enbolberloh parah regaloh*
Do you sell wrapping paper?	¿Venden papel de envolver? *benden papail day enbolbair*

un collar
oon koyar
necklace

una pulsera
oonah poolserah
bracelet

un reloj
oon reloh
watch

unos gemelos
oonos hemelos
cufflinks

una muñeca
oonah moonyekah
doll

un peluche
oon peloochay
soft toy

una cartera
oonah karterah
wallet

unos bombones
oonos bombonais
chocolates

Have you anything cheaper?	¿Tiene algo más barato? *tyenay algoh mas baratoh*
Is there a reduction for cash?	¿Hacen descuento por pago en efectivo? *ahthain deskwentoh por pagoh en efekteeboh*
Is there a guarantee?	¿Tiene garantía? *tyenay garantyah*
Can I exchange this?	¿Puedo descambiarlo? *pwedoh deskambyarloh*

You may hear...

- ¿Es para regalo?
  es parah regaloh
  Is it a present?

- ¿Se lo envuelvo para regalo?
  say loh enbwelboh parah regaloh
  Shall I gift-wrap it?

PHOTOGRAPHY

I'd like this film developed	Quisiera revelar este carrete *keesyera rebelar estay karretay*
When will it be ready?	¿Cuándo estará listo? *kwandoh estarah leestoh*
Do you have an express service?	¿Tiene servicio de revelado rápido? *tyenay serbeethyoh day rebeladoh rapeedoh*
I'd like the one-hour service	Quisiera el servicio de revelado en una hora *keesyera el serbeethyo day rebeladoh en oona ohrah*
I'd like a battery	Quisiera una pila *keesyera oonah peelah*

una cámara digital
oonah kamarah deeheetal
digital camera

una tarjeta de memoria
oonah tarhetah day memohryah
memory card

la película
lah peleekoolah
roll of film

un álbum de fotos
oon alboom day fohtos
photo album

un marco para fotos
oon markoh parah fohtos
photo frame

Do you print digital photos?	¿Imprimen fotos digitales? *eempreemen fohtos deeheetalais*
Can you print from this memory stick?	¿Puede imprimir de esta llave USB? *pweday eempreemeer day estah yabay oo essay bay*

un flash
oon flash
flash gun

una cámara
oonah kamarah
camera

un objetivo
oon obheteeboh
lens

una funda de la cámara
oonah foondah day lah kamarah
camera bag

You may hear...

- ¿Qué tamaño de fotos quiere?
  kay tamanyoh day fohtos kyeray
  What size prints do you want?

- ¿Mate o brillante?
  matay o breeyantay
  Matt or gloss?

- ¿Para cuándo las quiere?
  parah kwando las kyeray
  When do you want them?

AT THE POST OFFICE

I'd like...	Quisiera... *keesyerah*
...three stamps, please	...tres sellos, por favor *trais saiyos, por fabor*
...to register this letter	...certificar esta carta *therteefeekar estah kartah*
...to send this airmail	...enviar esto por avión *enbeear estoh por ahbyon*

un sobre
oon sobray
envelope

unos sellos
oonos sayos
stamps

una postal
oonah postal
postcard

por avión
por ahbyon
airmail

You may hear...

- **¿Qué contiene?**
  kay kontyenay
  What are the contents?

- **¿Qué valor tiene?**
  kay balor tyenay
  What is their value?

- **Rellene este impreso.**
  reyenay estay eempresoh
  Fill out this form.

How much is…?	¿Cuánto cuesta… _kwantoh kwestah_
…a letter to…	…enviar una carta a… _enbeear conah kartah ah_
…a postcard to…	…enviar una postal a… _enbeear conah postal ah_
…Great Britain	…Gran Bretaña _gran braitanyah_

un paquete
oon paketay
parcel

el mensajero
el mensaheroh
courier

un buzón
oon boothon
postbox

el cartero
el karteroh
postman

…the United States	…Estados Unidos _estados ocneedos_
…Canada	…Canadá _kanadah_
…Australia	…Australia _ah-oostralyah_
Can I have a receipt?	¿Me da un comprobante? _may dah oon komprobantay_
Where can I post this?	¿Dónde se echa esto al correo? _donday say echah estoh al korraio_

TELEPHONES

Where is the nearest phone box?

¿Dónde está la cabina más cercana?
donday estah lah kabeenah mas therkanah

el teléfono inalámbrico
el telefonoh eenalambreekoh
cordless phone

el móvil
el mobeel
mobile phone

la tarjeta telefónica
la tarhetah telefohneekah
phone card

la cabina
lah kabeenah
telephone box

el teléfono de monedas
el telefonoh day monedas
coin phone

el contestador automático
el kontestador ah-ootomateekoh
answering machine

Who's speaking?	¿Quién llama? *kyen yamah*
Hello, this is…	Hola, soy… *ohlah soy*
I'd like to speak to…	Quisiera hablar con… *keesyerah ahblar kon*
Can I leave a message?	¿Puedo dejarle un mensaje? *pwedoh deharlay oon mensahay*

INTERNET

Is there an internet café near here?	¿Hay un cibercafé por aquí cerca? *ah-ee oon theebercafay por ahkee therkah*
How much do you charge?	¿Cuánto cobran? *kwantoh kobran*
Do you have wireless internet?	¿Tienen conexión inalámbrica a Internet? *tyenain koneksyon eenalambreekah ah internet*
Can I check my emails?	¿Puedo comprobar mis emails? *pwedoh komporbar mees eemaeels*
I need to send an email	Tengo que enviar un email *taingoh kay enbeear oon eemaeel*
What's your email address?	¿Cuál es su dirección de email? *kwal es soo deerekthyon day eemaeel*
My email address is...	Mi dirección de email es... *mee deerekthyon day eemaeel es*

el portátil
el portateel
laptop

el teclado
el tekladoh
keyboard

el sitio web
el seetyo web
website

el email
el eemaeel
email

SIGHTSEEING

Most towns have a tourist information office and the staff will advise you on local places to visit and excursions. Many museums and art galleries close on Mondays as well as public holidays, so check the opening times before visiting. You will usually have to pay an admission fee, but some offer discounts to seniors, minors and students.

AT THE TOURIST OFFICE

Where is the tourist information office?	¿Dónde está la oficina de turismo? *donday estah clah ofeetheenah dey tooreesmoh*
Can you recommend...	¿Puede recomendarme... *pweday raikomendarmay*
...a guided tour?	...una visita guiada? *oonah beeseetah geeyadah*
...an excursion?	...una excursión? *oonah ekskoorsyon*
Is there a museum or art gallery?	¿Hay un museo o una galería de arte? *ah-ee con moosayoh oh oonah galereeyah day artay*
Is it open to the public?	¿Está abierto al público? *estah ahbyertoh al poobleekoh*
Is there wheelchair access?	¿Dispone de acceso para sillas de ruedas? *deesponay day akthaisoh parah seeyas day rwedas*
Does it close...	¿Cierra... *thyerah*
...on Sundays?	...los domingos? *los dohmeengos*
...on bank holidays?	...los festivos? *los festeebos*
How long does it take to get there?	¿Cuánto se tarda en llegar? *kwantoh say tardah en yegar*
Do you have...	¿Tiene... *tyenay*
...a street map?	...un plano? *oon plahnoh*
...a guide?	...una guía? *oonah gheeyah*
...any leaflets?	...folletos? *fohyetos*

VISITING PLACES

| What time… | ¿A qué hora… |
| | *ah kay ohrah* |

| …do you open? | …abren? |
| | *ahbrain* |

| …do you close? | …cierran? |
| | *thyerran* |

| I'd like two entrance tickets | Quisiera dos entradas |
| | *keesyerah dos entradas* |

| Two adults, please | Dos adultos, por favor |
| | *dos ahdooltos por fabor* |

| A family ticket, please | Una entrada familiar |
| | *oonah entradah fameelyar* |

| How much does it cost? | ¿Cuánto cuesta? |
| | *kwantoh kwestah* |

| Are there reductions for… | ¿Hacen descuento a… |
| | *ahthain deskwentoh ah* |

| …children? | …los niños? |
| | *los neenyos* |

| …students? | …los estudiantes? |
| | *los estoodyantais* |

el plano
el planoh
street map

la oficina de turismo
lah ofeetheenah day tooreesmoh
tourist office

el acceso para sillas de ruedas
el akthaisoh parah seeyas day rwedas
wheelchair access

Can I buy a guidebook?	¿Puedo comprar una guía? *pwedoh komprar oonah gheeyah*
Is there...	¿Hay... *ah-ee*
...an audio-guide?	...guías en audio? *gheeyas en ah-oodyo*
...a guided tour?	...una visita guiada? *oonah beeseetah gheeyadah*
...a lift?	...un ascensor? *oon asthensor*
...a bus tour?	...una excursión en autocar? *oonah ekskoorsyon en ah-ootocar*
...wheelchair access?	acceso para sillas de ruedas? *akthaisoh parah seeyas dow rwedas*
...a gift shop?	...una tienda de regalos? *oonah tyendah day regalos*

el autobús turístico
el ah-ootoboos tooreesteekoh
tour bus

You may hear...

• ¿Tiene carné de estudiante?
tyenay karnay day estoodyantay
Do you have a student card?

FINDING YOUR WAY

Excuse me	Disculpe *deeskoolpay*
Can you help me?	¿Puede ayudarme? *pweday ahyoodarmay*
Is this the way to...?	¿Por aquí se va... *por ahkee say bah*
How do I get to...?	¿Cómo se va... *komoh say bah*
...the town centre?	...al centro? *al thentroh*
...the station?	...a la estación? *ah lah estathyon*
...the museum?	...al museo? *al moosayoh*
...the art gallery?	...a la galería de arte? *ah lah galereeyah day artay*
How long does it take?	¿Cuánto se tarda? *kwantoh say tardah*
Is it far?	¿Está lejos? *estah lehos*
Is it within walking distance?	¿Se puede ir andando? *say pweday eer andandoh*
Can you show me on the map?	¿Puede indicármelo en el plano? *pweday eendeekarmeloh en el planoh*

You may hear...

- **No está lejos.**
  noh estah lehos
  It's not far away.

- **Se tardan diez minutos.**
  say tardan deeyaith meenootos
  It takes ten minutes.

You may hear...

- **Estamos aquí**
  estamos ahkee — We are here

- **Siga todo recto...**
  seegah todoh rektoh — Keep straight on...

- **...hasta el final de la calle**
  astah el feenal day lah kayay — ...to the end of the street

- **...hasta el semáforo**
  astah el saimaforoh — ...to the traffic lights

- **...hasta la plaza**
  astah lah plathah — ...to the main square

- **Por aquí**
  por ahkee — This way

- **Por allí**
  por ahyee — That way

- **Doble a la derecha en...**
  doblay ah lah derechah en — Turn right at...

- **Doble a la izquierda en...**
  doblay ah lah eethkyerdah en — Turn left at

- **Coja la primera...**
  kohah lah preemerah — Take the first...

- **...a la izquierda/derecha**
  ah lah eethkyerdah/derechah — ...on the left/right

- **Queda delante de usted**
  kedah dailantay day oosted — It's in front of you

- **Queda detrás de usted**
  kedah detras day oosted — It's behind you

- **Queda enfrente de usted**
  kedah ainfrentay day oosted — It's opposite you

- **Está al lado de...**
  estah al ladoh day — It's next to...

- **Está señalizado**
  estah senyaleethadoh — It's signposted

- **Está por alli**
  estah por ahyee — It's over there

PLACES TO VISIT

el ayuntamiento
el ah-yoontamyentoh
town hall

el puente
el pwentay
bridge

el museo
el moosayoh
museum

la galería de arte
lah galereeyah day artay
art gallery

el monumento
el monoomentoh
monument

la iglesia
la eeglesya
church

la catedral
lah kataydral
cathedral

el pueblo
el pwebloh
village

el parque
el parkay
park

el puerto
el pwertoh
harbour

el faro
el faroh
lighthouse

los viñedos
los beenyedos
vineyard

el castillo
el kasteeyoh
castle

la costa
la kostah
coast

la cascada
lah kaskadah
waterfall

las montañas
las montanyas
mountains

OUTDOOR ACTIVITIES

Where can we go…	¿Dónde podemos ir… *donday podemos eer*
…horse riding?	…a montar a caballo? *ah montar ah kabayoh*
…fishing?	…a pescar? *ah peskar*
…swimming?	…a nadar? *ah nadar*
…walking?	…a pasear? *ah pasaiar*
Can we…	¿Podemos… *podemos*
…hire equipment?	…alquilar el equipo? *alkeelar el ekeepoh*
…have lessons?	…tomar clases? *tomar klasais*
How much per hour?	¿Cuánto cuesta a la hora? *kwantoh kwestah ah lah ohrah*
I'm a beginner	Soy principiante *soy preentheepyantay*
I'm quite experienced	Tengo bastante experiencia *taingoh bastantay eksperyenthya*
Where's the amusement park?	¿Dónde está el parque de atracciones? *donday estah el parkay day atrakthyonais*
Can the children go on all the rides?	¿Los niños pueden subirse en todas las atracciones? *los neenyos pweden soobeersay en todas las atrakthyonais*
Is there a playground?	¿Hay columpios? *ah-ee koloompyos*
Is it safe for children?	¿Es seguro para los niños? *es segooroh parah los neenyos*

el parque de atracciones
el parkay day atrakthyonais
fairground

el parque temático
el parkay taimateekoh
theme park

el safari
el safaree
safari park

el zoológico
el tho-ohloheekoh
zoo

los columpios
los koloompyos
playground

el picnic
el peekneek
picnic

la pesca
la peskah
fishing

montar a caballo
montar ah kabayoh
horse riding

SPORTS AND LEISURE

Spain can offer the traveller a wide range of cultural events, musical entertainments, leisure activities and sports. You can swim or enjoy a range of watersports on the coast, hike, cycle or ride in the national parks, or even go skiing in the mountains. Spain has some of the best golf courses in the world, especially on the sunny Costa del Sol. Although you rarely need to be a club member to play a round, it can be quite expensive on the most famous courses

LEISURE TIME

I like...	Me gusta... *may goostah*
...art and painting	...el arte y la pintura *el artay ee lah peentoorah*
...films and cinema	...las películas y el cine *las peleekoolas ee el theenay*
...the theatre	...el teatro *el tay-ahtroh*
...opera	...la ópera *lah ohperah*
I prefer...	Prefiero... *prefeeroh*
...reading books	...leer libros *lay-air leebros*
...listening to music	...escuchar música *eskoochar mooseekah*
...watching sport	...ver deporte *bair deportay*
...playing games	...jugar a juegos *hoogar ah hoo-engos*
...going to concerts	...ir a conciertos *eer ah konthyertos*
...dancing	...bailar *bah-eeyiar*
...going clubbing	...ir de discotecas *eer day dyskotekas*
...going out with friends	...salir con los amigos *saleer kon los ahmeegos*
I don't like...	No me gusta... *noh may goostah*
That bores me	Eso me aburre *esoh may ahboorav*
That doesn't interest me	Eso no me interesa *esoh noh may eenteresah*

AT THE BEACH

Can I hire...	¿Puedo alquilar... *pwedoh alkeelar*
...a jet ski?	...una moto acuática? *oonah motoh akwateekah*
...a beach umbrella?	...un parasol? *oon parasol*
...a surfboard?	...una tabla de surf? *oonah tablah day soorf*
...a wetsuit?	...un traje de neopreno? *oon trahay day nayoprenoh*

la toalla de playa
lah toah-yah day playah
beach towel

la pelota hinchable
lah pelotah eenchablay
beach ball

la hamaca
lah ahmakah
deck chair

la tumbona
lah toombonah
sun lounger

You may hear...

- **Prohibido bañarse.**
  proybeedoh banyarsay
  Don't swim.

- **Playa cerrada.**
  playah theradah
  Beach closed.

- **Fuertes corrientes.**
  fwertais koryentais
  Strong currents.

las gafas de sol
las gafas day sol
sunglasses

el sombrero
el sombreroh
sunhat

el bikini
el beekeenee
bikini

el bronceador
el bronthechdor
suntan lotion

las aletas
las ahlaitas
flippers

las gafas y el tubo de buceo
las gafas ee el tooboh day boothaio
mask and snorkel

How much does it cost?	¿Cuánto cuesta? *kwanto kwestah*
Can I go water-skiing?	¿Puedo hacer esquí acuático? *pwedoh ahthair eskee akwateekoh*
Is there a lifeguard?	¿Hay socorristas? *ah-ee sokoreestas*
Is it safe to...	¿Es seguro... *es segooroh*
...swim here?	...bañarse aquí? *banyarsay ahkee*
...surf here?	...hacer surf aquí? *ahthair soorf ahkee*

AT THE SWIMMING POOL

What time…	¿A qué hora…
	ah kay ohrah
…does the pool open?	…abre la piscina?
	abray lah peestheenah
…does the pool close?	…cierra la piscina?
	thyerah lah peestheenah
Is it…	¿Hay…
	ah-ee
…an indoor pool?	…piscina cubierta?
	peestheenah koobyertah
…an outdoor pool?	…piscina descubierta?
	peestheenah deskoobyertah
Is there a children's pool?	¿Hay piscina infantil?
	ah-ee peestheenah eenfanteel
Where are the changing rooms?	¿Dónde están los vestuarios?
	donday estan los bestwaryos
Is it safe to dive?	¿Es seguro tirarse desde el trampolín?
	es segooroh teerarsay dezday el trampoleen

los manguitos
los mangheetos
armband

los flotadores
los flohtadohres
float

las gafas de natación
las gafas day natathyon
swimming goggles

el bañador
el banyador
swimsuit

AT THE GYM

la máquina de remo
lah makeenah day raimoh
rowing machine

la bicicleta elíptica
lah beetheekletah eleepteekah
cross trainer

el stepper
el esteppair
step machine

la bicicleta estática
lah beetheekletah estateekah
exercise bike

Is there a gym?	¿Hay gimnasio? *ah-ee heemnasyo*
Is it free for guests?	¿Es gratis para los huéspedes? *es gratees parah los wespedais*
What amenities does it offer?	¿Qué servicios ofrece? *kay serbeethyos ofrethay*
Do I have to wear trainers?	¿Tengo que llevar bambas? *taingoh kay yebar bambas*
Do I need an induction session?	¿Es necesaria una sesión de introducción? *es nethesaryah oonah sesyon day eentrodookthyon*
Do you hold...	¿Dan... *dan*
...aerobics classes?	...clases de aeróbic? *klasais day aherobeek*
...Pilates classes?	...clases de Pilates? *klasais day peelatais*
...yoga classes?	...clases de yoga? *klasais day yohgah*

BOATING AND SAILING

Can I hire...	¿Puedo alquilar... *pwedoh alkeelar*
...a dinghy?	...un bote? *oon botay*
...a windsurfer?	...una tabla de windsurf? *oonah tablah day windsoorf*
...a canoe?	...una canoa? *oonah kanoah*

el chaleco salvavidas
el chalaikoh salbabeedas
life jacket

la brújula
lah broohoolah
compass

...a rowing boat?	...una barca de remos *oonah barkah day raimos*
Do you offer sailing lessons?	¿Dan clases de navegación? *dan klasais day nabegathyon*
Do you have a mooring?	¿Tienen atracadero? *tyenain ahtrakadairoh*
How much is it for the night?	¿Cuánto cuesta por noche? *kwantoh kwestah por nochay*
Where can I buy gas?	¿Dónde se puede comprar el gas? *donday say pweday komprar el gas*
Where is the marina?	¿Dónde está el puerto deportivo? *donday estah el pwertoh deporteeboh*
Are there life jackets?	¿Hay chalecos salvavidas? *ah-ee chalekos salbabeedas*

WINTER SPORTS

I would like to hire...	Quisiera alquilar... *keesyerah alkeelar*
...some skis	...unos esquíes *oonos eskyes*
...some ski boots	...unas botas de esquí *oonas bohtas day eskee*
...some poles	...unos bastones *oonos bastonais*
...a snowboard	...una tabla de snowboard *oonah tablah day esnowbord*
...a helmet	...un casco *oon kaskoh*
When does...	¿Cuándo... *Kwandoh*
...the chair lift start?	...empieza el te esilla? *empyethah el teleseeyah*
...the cable car finish?	...acaba el teleférico? *akabah el telefereekoh*
How much is a lift pass?	¿Cuánto cuesta un pase para el te esilla? *kwantoh kwestah oon pasay parah el teleseeyah*
Can I take skiing lessons?	¿Puedo tomar clases de esquí? *pwedoh tomar klasais day eskee*

You may hear...

- ¿Es usted principiante?
  es oosted preentheepyanteh
  Are you a beginner?

- Hay que abonar una paga y señal.
  ah-ee kay ahbonar oonah pagah ee sainyal
  I need a deposit.

BALL GAMES

I like playing…	Me gusta jugar… *may goostah hoogar*
…football	…al fútbol *al footbol*
…tennis	…al tenis *al tenees*
…golf	…al golf *al golf*
…badminton	…al bádminton *al badmeenton*
…squash	…al squash *al eskwash*
Where is the nearest…	¿Dónde está… *donday estah*
…tennis court?	…la pista de tenis más cercana? *lah peestah day tenees mas therkanah*
…golf course?	…el campo de golf más cercano? *el kampoh day golf mas therkanoh*

el balón de fútbol
el balón day footbol
football

las muñequeras
las moonyekeras
wristbands

la canasta
lah kanastah
basket

el guante de béisbol
el wantay day beysbol
baseball mitt

Can I book a court…	¿Puedo reservar una pista… *pwedoh reserbar oonah* *peestah*
…for two hours?	…para dos horas? *parah dos ohras*
…at three o'clock?	…a las tres? *ah las trais*
What shoes are allowed?	¿Qué calzado está permitido? *kay kalthadoh estah* *permeeteedoh*
Can I hire…	¿Puedo alquilar… *pwedoh alkeelar*
…a tennis racquet?	…una raqueta de tenis? *oonah rakaitah day tenees*
…some balls?	…pelotas? *pailotas*
…a set of clubs?	…un juego de palos? *oon hoo-egoh day pahlos*
…a golf buggy?	…un buggy? *oon buggy*

la raqueta de tenis
lah rakaitah day tenees
tennis racquet

las pelotas de tenis
las pailotas day tenees
tennis balls

la pelota y el tee de golf
lah pelotah ee el tee day golf
golf ball and tee

el palo de golf
el panloh day golf
golf club

GOING OUT

Where is…	¿Dónde está… *donday estah*
…the opera house?	…el teatro de la ópera? *el tay-ahtroh day lah ohperah*
…a jazz club?	…un club de jazz? *oon kloob day jazz*
Do I have to book in advance?	¿Tengo que reservar con antelación? *Taingoh kay reserbar kon antelathyon*
I'd like…tickets	Deme…entradas *daymay…entradas*
I'd like seats…	Quisiera los asientos… *keesyerah los asyentos*
…at the back	…en el fondo *en el fondoh*
…at the front	…delante *daylantay*
…in the middle	…en el centro *en el thentroh*
…in the gallery	…en el gallinero *en el gayeeneroh*
Can I buy a programme?	¿Puedo comprar un programa? *Pwedoh komprar oon programah*

You may hear…

- **Apaguen los móviles.**
  Apaghen los mobeelais
  Turn off your mobiles.

- **Regresen a sus asientos.**
  Raygresain ah soos ahsyentos
  Return to your seats.

el teatro
el tay-ahtroh
theatre

el teatro de la ópera
el tay-ahtroh day lah ohpe-rah
opera house

el músico
el mooseekoh
musician

el pianista
el pyaneestah
pianist

el cantante
el kantantay
singer

el ballet
el baleh
ballet

el cine
el theenay
cinema

las palomitas de maíz
las palomeetas day ma-eeth
popcorn

el casino
el kaseenoh
casino

el club nocturno
el kloob noktoornoh
nightclub

GALLERIES AND MUSEUMS

What are the opening hours?	¿Qué horario tiene? *kay ohraryoh tyenay*
Are there guided tours in English?	¿Hay visitas guiadas en inglés? *ah-ee beeseetas gheeyadas en eenglais*
When does the tour leave?	¿De dónde parte el recorrido? *day donday partay el rekorreedoh*
How much does it cost?	¿Cuánto cuesta? *kwantoh kwestah*
How long does it take?	¿Cuánto dura? *kwantoh doorah*
Do you have an audio guide?	¿Tienen una guía en audio? *tyenen oonah gheeya en ah-oodyoh*
Do you have a guidebook in English?	¿Tienen una guía en inglés? *tyenen oonah gheeya en eenglais*
Is (flash) photography allowed?	¿Permiten hacer fotos (con flash)? *permeetain ahthair fotos (kon flash)*

la estatua
lah estatwa
statue

el busto
el boostoh
bust

Can you direct me to…?	¿Puede indicarme el camino a…? *pweday eendeekarmay el kameenoh ah*
I'd really like to see…	Me gustaría ver… *may goostarya ber*
Who painted this?	¿Quién ha pintado esto? *kyen ah peentadoh estoh*
How old is it?	¿Cuántos años hace? *kwantos anyos ahthay*

la pintura
lah peentoorah
painting

el grabado
el grabadoh
engraving

el dibujo
el deeboohoh
drawing

el manuscrito
el manooscreetoh
manuscript

Are there wheelchair ramps?	¿Hay rampas para sillas de ruedas? *ah-ee rampas parah seeyas day rwedas*
Is there a lift?	¿Hay ascensor? *ah-ee asthensor*
Where are the toilets?	¿Dónde están los aseos? *donday están los ahsaios*
I've lost my group	He perdido a mi grupo *eh perdeedoh ah mee groopoh*

HOME ENTERTAINMENT

How do I...	¿Cómo se... *komoh say*
...turn the television on?	...enciende el televisor? *enthyenday el telebeesor*
...change channels?	...cambian los canales? *kambyan los kanalais*
...turn the volume up?	...le sube el volumen? *lay soobay el boloomain*
...turn the volume down?	...le baja el volumen? *lay bahah el boloomain*
Do you have satellite TV?	¿Tiene televisión por satélite? *tyenay telebeesyon por sateleetay*
Where can I buy...	¿Dónde se puede comprar... *donday say pweday komprar*
...a DVD?	...un DVD? *oon dayoobeday*
...a music CD?	...un CD de música? *oon thay day day mooseekah*

el televisor de pantalla ancha
el telebeesor day pantayah anchah
widescreen TV

el reproductor de DVD
el reprodooktor day dayoobeday
DVD player

el mando a distancia
el mandoh ah deestanthya
remote control

el videojuego
el beedaiohoo-aygoh
video game

el reproductor de CD
el reprodooktor day thaidc/s
CD player

el iPod
el eepod
iPod

la radio
lah rahdyo
radio

el portátil
el portateel
laptop

el ratón
el raton
mouse

Can I use this to…	¿Puedo usar esto para… *pwedoh oosar estoh parah*
…go online?	…conectarme a Internet? *konektarmay ah internet*
Is it broadband/wifi?	¿Es banda ancha/wifi? *es bandah anchah/weefee*
How do I…	¿Cómo… *komoh*
…log on?	…inicio sesión? *eeneethyo sesyon*
…log out?	…cierro sesión? *thyerroh sesyon*
…reboot?	…reinicio? *reh-eeneethyo*

HEALTH

If you are an EU national, you are entitled to free emergency medical treatment in Spain, but you will have to produce your European Health Insurance Card. It is a good idea to familiarize yourself with a few basic phrases for use in an emergency or in case you need to go into a pharmacy or visit a doctor, dentist or hospital.

USEFUL PHRASES

I need a doctor	Necesito un médico *netheseetoh oon medeekoh*
I would like an appointment...	Quisiera que me dieran hora... *keesyerah kay may deeyehran ohrah*
...as soon as possible	...lo antes posible *loh antais poseeblay*
...today	...para hoy *parah oi*
...tomorrow	...para mañana *parah manyanah*
It's very urgent	Es muy urgente *es mooy oorhentay*
I have a European Health Insurance Card	Tengo la tarjeta del seguro europeo *taingoh lah tarhetah dail segooroh eh-ooropaioh*
I have health insurance	Tengo seguro médico *taingoh segooroh medeekoh*
Can I have a receipt?	¿Me puede dar un comprobante? *may pweday dar oon komprobantay*
Where is the nearest...	¿Dónde está... *donday estah*
...pharmacy?	...la farmacia más cercana? *lah farmatheeya mas therkanah*
...doctor's surgery?	...el ambulatorio más cercano? *el amboolatoryo mas therkanoh*
...hospital?	...el hospital más cercano? *el ospeetal mas therkanoh*
...dentist?	...el dentista más cercano? *el denteestah mas therkanoh*

AT THE PHARMACY

What can I take for…?	¿Qué me puedo tomar para…? *kay may pwedoh tomar parah*
How many should I take?	¿Cuántos tengo que tomar? *Kwantos taingoh kay tomar*
Is it safe for children?	¿Se les puede dar a los niños? *say lais pweday dar ah los neenyos*
Are there side effects?	¿Tiene efectos secundarios? *tyenay aifektos sekoondaryos*
Do you have that…	¿Lo tiene en… *loh tyenay en*
…as tablets?	…pastillas? *pasteeyas*
…in capsule form?	…en cápsulas? *en kapsoolas*
I'm allergic to…	Soy alérgico a… *soy alerheekoh ah*
I'm already taking…	Ya estoy tomando… *ya estoy tomandoh*
Do I need a prescription?	¿Necesito una receta? *netheseetoh oonah rethetah*

You may hear...

- **Tómese esto…veces al día.**
  tomesay estoh…bethays al deeyah
  Take this…times a day.

- **Antes de comer.**
  antais day komair
  Before eating.

- **Con la comida.**
  kon lah komeedah
  With food.

la venda
lah bendah
bandage

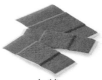

la tirita
lah teereetah
plaster

las cápsulas
las kapsoolas
capsules

las pastillas
las pasteeyas
pills

el inhalador
el eenalador
inhaler

el supositorio
el sooposeetoryo
suppository

las gotas
las gohtas
drops

el aerosol
el aehrosol
spray

la pomada
lah pohmadah
ointment

el jarabe
el harabay
syrup

THE HUMAN BODY

I have hurt my...	Me he hecho daño en el... *may hay aicho danyo en el*
I have cut my...	Me he cortado el... *may hay kortadoh el*

el codo
el kodoh
elbow

el brazo
el brathoh
arm

la cabeza
lah kabaithah
head

el hombro
el ombroh
shoulder

el cuello
el kweyoh
neck

el pecho
el paichoh
chest

el estómago
el estomagoh
stomach

la pierna
lah pyernah
leg

la rodilla
lah rodeeyah
knee

el pie
el pee-ay
foot

FACE

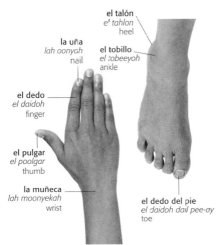

la piel
lah pyel
skin

la oreja
lah oraihah
ear

el lunar
el loonar
mole

la barbilla
lah barbeeyah
chin

el ojo
el ohoh
eye

la mejilla
lah meheeyah
cheek

la mandíbula
lah mandeeboolah
jaw

la boca
lah bokah
mouth

la nariz
lah nareeth
nose

HAND

FOOT

el talón
el tahlon
heel

el tobillo
el tobeeyoh
ankle

la uña
lah oonyah
nail

el dedo
el daidoh
finger

el pulgar
el poolgar
thumb

la muñeca
lah moonyekah
wrist

el dedo del pie
el daidoh dail pee-ay
toe

FEELING ILL

I don't feel well	No me encuentro bien *noh may enkwentroh byen*
I feel ill	Estoy enfermo *estoy ainfermoh*
I have...	Tengo... *taingoh*
...an ear ache	...dolor de oídos *dolor day o-eedos*
...a stomach ache	...dolor de estómago *dolor day estomagoh*
...a sore throat	...dolor de garganta *dolor day gargantah*
...a temperature	...fiebre *feeyebreh*
...hayfever	...alergia al polen *alerhyah al pohlain*
...constipation	...estreñimiento *estrenyeemyentoh*
...diarrhoea	...diarrea *dyarraiah*
...toothache	...dolor de muelas *dolor day moo-ailas*
I've been stung by...	Me ha picado... *may ah peekadoh*
...a bee/wasp	...una abeja/una avispa *oonah abehah/oonah abeespah*
...a jellyfish	...una medusa *oonah medoosah*
I've been bitten by...	Me ha mordido... *may ah mordeedoh*
...a snake	...una serpiente *oonah serpyentay*
...a dog	...un perro *oon perroh*

INJURIES

el corte
el kortay
cut

el rasguño
el rasgoonyoh
graze

el cardenal
el kardainai
bruise

la astilla
lah asteeyah
splinter

la quemadura de sol
lah kaimadoorah day sol
sunburn

la quemadura
lah kaimadoorah
burn

la mordedura
lah mordedoorah
bite

la picadura
lah peekadoorah
sting

el esguince
el esgheenthay
sprain

la fractura
lah fraktoorah
fracture

AT THE DOCTOR

I'm...	Estoy... *Estoy*
...vomiting	...vomitando *bomeetandoh*
...bleeding	...sangrando *sangrandoh*
...dizzy	...mareado/a *maraiadoh/ah*
...feeling faint	...desmayándome *daismayandomay*
...pregnant	...embarazada *embarathadah*
...diabetic	...diabético/a *deeyabeteekoh/ah*
...epileptic	...epiléptico/a *epeelepteekoh/ah*
I have...	Tengo... *taingoh*
...arthritis	...artritis *artreetees*
...a heart condition	...una enfermedad cardíaca *oonah ainfermedad kardyakah*
...high blood pressure	...la presión alta *lah presyon altah*

You may hear...

- ¿Qué le pasa?
  kay lay pasah
  What's wrong?

- ¿Dónde le duele?
  donday lay dweleh
  Where does it hurt?

ILLNESS

el dolor de cabeza
el dolor day kabaithah
headache

la hemorragia nasal
lah emorrahya nasal
nosebleed

la tos
lah tos
cough

el estornudo
el estornoodoh
sneeze

el resfriado
el resfreeyadoh
cold

la gripe
lah greepay
flu

el asma
el asmah
asthma

el calambre
el kalambray
stomach cramps

la náusea
lah naoosaia
nausea

el sarpullido
el sarpooyeedoh
rash

AT THE HOSPITAL

Can you help me?	¿Puede ayudarme? *pweday ahyoodarmay*
I need…	Necesito… *netheseetoh*
…a doctor	…un médico *oon medeekoh*
…a nurse	…una enfermera *oonah ainfermerah*
Where is…	¿Dónde está… *donday estah*
…the accident and emergency department?	…urgencias? *oorhenthyas*
…the children's ward?	…la sala de pediatría? *lah salah day paidyatrya*
…the X-ray department?	…el departamento de las radiografías? *el daipartamentoh day las radyografyas*
…the waiting room?	…la sala de urgencias? *lah salah day oorhenthyas*

la inyección
lah eenjekthyon
injection

el análisis de sangre
el analeesees day sangray
blood test

la radiografía
lah radyografya
X-ray

el escáner
el eskanair
scan

...the intensive care unit?	...la unidad de cuidados intensivos? *lah ooneedad day kweedados eentenseebos*
...the lift/stairs?	...el ascensor/ las escaleras? *el asthensor/las eskaleras*
I think I've broken...	Creo que me he roto... *krai-oh kay may eh rotoh*
Do I need...	¿Necesito... *netheseetoh*
...an injection?	...una inyección? *oonah eenjekthyon*
...antibiotics?	...antibióticos? *anteebeeyoteekos*
...an operation?	...una operación? *oonah ohperathyon*
Will it hurt?	¿Me dolerá? *may dolerah*
How long will it take?	¿Cuánto durará? *kwantoh doorarah*

la silla de ruedas
lah seeyah day rwedas
wheelchair

el boca a boca
el bokah ah bokah
resuscitation

la tablilla
lah tableeyah
splint

el vendaje
el bendahay
dressing

EMERGENCIES

In an emergency, dial 061 for an ambulance (*una ambulancia*) or the pan-European number 112 for the fire brigade (*los bomberos*), or 092 for the local police (*la policía*). However, numbers do vary in different regions, so check this out locally. If you are the victim of a crime or you lose your passport, money or other possessions, you should report the incident to the police without delay.

IN AN EMERGENCY

Help!	¡Socorro! *sokorroh*
Please go away!	¡Váyase! *byasay*
Let go!	¡Suélteme! *sweltemay*
Stop! Thief!	¡Alto! ¡Al ladrón! *altoh al ladron*
Call the police!	¡Llamen a la policía! *yamain ah lah politheeya*
Get a doctor!	¡Llamen a un médico! *yamain ah oon medeekoh*
I need...	Necesito... *netheseetoh*
...the police	...a la policía *ah lah politheeya*
...the fire brigade	...a los bomberos *ah los bomberos*
...an ambulance	...una ambulancia *oonah amboolanthya*
It's very urgent	Es muy urgente *es mooy oorhentay*
Where is...	¿Dónde está... *donday estah*
...the British embassy?	...la embajada británica? *lah embahadah breetaneekah*
...the British consul?	...el consulado británico? *el konsooladoh breetaneekoh*
...the police station?	...la comisaría? *lah komeesarya*
...the hospital?	...el hospital? *el ospeetal*

ACCIDENTS

I need to make a telephone call	Tengo que llamar por teléfono *taingoh kay yamar por telefonoh*
I'd like to report an accident	Quiero informar de un accidente *kyeroh eenformar day oon aktheedentay*
I've crashed my car	He chocado con el coche *eh chokadoh kon el kochay*
The registration number is...	La matrícula es... *lah matreekoolah es*
I'm at...	Estoy en... *estoy en*
Please come quickly!	¡Vengan rápido, por favor! *baingan rapeedoh por fabor*
Someone's injured	Hay heridos *ah-ee ehreedos*
Someone's been knocked down	Ha habido un atropello *ah abeedoh oon atropeyoh*
There's a fire at...	Hay un incendio en... *ah-ee oon eenthendyo en*
Someone is trapped in the building	Hay alguien atrapado en el edificio *ah-ee alghyen atrapadoh en el edeefeethyo*

You may hear...

- ¿Qué servicio precisa?
  kay serbeethyo praytheesah
  Which service do you require?

- ¿Qué ha pasado?
  kay ah pasadoh
  What happened?

EMERGENCY SERVICES

la ambulancia
lah amboolanthya
ambulance

los bomberos
los bomberos
firefighters

el camión de bomberos
el kamyon day bomberos
fire engine

la alarma de incendios
lah alarmah day eerthendyos
fire alarm

la boca de riego
lah bokah day reeyegoh
hydrant

el extintor
el eksteentor
fire extinguisher

las esposas
las aisposas
handcuffs

el coche patrulla
el kochay patrooyah
police car

el policía
el politheeya
policeman

POLICE AND CRIME

I want to report a crime	Quiero poner una denuncia *kyeroh ponair oonah denoonthya*
I've been...	Me han... *may ahn*
...robbed	...asaltado *asaltadoh*
...attacked	...atacado *atakadoh*
...mugged	...atracado *atrakadoh*
...raped	...violado *beeyoladoh*
...burgled	...robado *robadoh*
Someone has stolen...	Me han robado... *may ahn robadoh*
...my car	...el coche *el kochay*
...my money	...el dinero *el deeneroh*
...my traveller's cheques	...los cheques de viaje *los chekais day beeyahay*
...my passport	...el pasaporte *el pasaportay*

You may hear...

- ¿Cuándo ha pasado? *kwandoh ah pasadoh* When did it happen?

- ¿Hay testigos? *ah-ee testeegos* Was there a witness?

- ¿Qué aspecto tenía? *kay aspektoh tainya* What did he look like?

I'd like to speak to…	Quiero hablar con… *kyeroh ahblar kon*
…a senior officer	…un superior *oon sooperyor*
…a policewoman	…una muher policía *oonah moohair politheeya*
I need…	Necesito… *netheseetoh*
…a lawyer	…un abogado *oon abogadoh*
…an interpreter	…un intérprete *oon eenterpretay*
…to make a phone call	…hacer una llamada *ahthair oonah yamadah*
I'm very sorry, officer	Lo siento mucho, agente *loh syentoh moochoh ahentay*
Here is…	Aquí tiene… *ahkee tyenay*
…my driving licence	…mi carné de conducir *mee karnay day kondootheer*
…my insurance	…mi seguro *mee segooroh*
How much is the fine?	¿Cuánto es la multa? *kwantoh es lah mooltah*

You may hear…

- Su carné de conducir, por favor. *soo karnay day kondootheer, por fabor* Your licence, please.

- Sus papeles, por favor. *soos papailays por fabor* Your papers, please.

AT THE GARAGE

Where is the nearest garage?	¿Dónde está el taller mecánico más cercano? *donday estah el tayair mekaneekoh mas therkanoh*
Can you do repairs?	¿Hace reparaciones? *ahthay rayparathyones*
I need...	Necesito... *netheseetoh*
...a new tyre	...que cambie el neumático *kay kambeeyay el nayoomateekoha*
...a new exhaust	...que cambie el tubo de escape *kay kambeeyay el tooboh day eskapay*
...a new windscreen	...que cambie el parabrisas *kay kambeeyay el parabreesas*
...a new bulb	...que cambie la bombilla *kay kambeeyay lah bombeeyah*
...wiper blades	...limpiaparabrisas *leempyaparabreesas*
Do you have one in stock?	¿Tiene alguno aquí? *tyenay algoonoh ahkee*
Can you replace this?	¿Puede cambiar esto? *pweday kambyar estoh*
The...is not working	El...no funciona *el...noh foonthyonah*
There is something wrong with the engine	Le pasa algo al motor *lay pasah algoh al mohtor*
How long will it take?	¿Cuánto tardará? *kwantoh tardarah*
When will it be ready?	¿Cuándo estará listo? *kwandoh estarah leestoh*
How much will it cost?	¿Cuánto costará? *kwantoh kostarah*

CAR BREAKDOWN

My car has broken down	Se me ha averiado el coche *say may ah aberyadoh el kochay*
Please can you help me?	¿Puede ayudarme, por favor? *pweday ahyoodarmay por fabor*
Please come to...	Por favor, venga a... *por fabor bengah ah*
I have a puncture	Se me ha pinchado una rueda *say may ah peenchadoh oonah rwedah*
Can you help change the wheel?	¿Puede ayudarme a cambiar la rueda? *pweday ahyoodarmay ah kambeeyar lah rwedah*
I need a new tyre	Necesito un neumático nuevo *netheseetoh oon nayoomateekoh noo-eboh*
My car won't start	El coche no arranca *el kochay noh arankah*
The engine is overheating	El motor se ha recalentado *el mohtor say ah rekalentadoh*
Can you fix it?	¿Puede arreglarlo? *pweday arreglarloh*

You may hear...

- ¿Necesita ayuda?
  netheseetah ahyoodah
  Do you need any help?

- ¿Lleva rueda de repuesto?
  yaybah rwedah day repwestoh
  Do you have a spare tyre?

LOST PROPERTY

I've lost…	He perdido… *eh perdeedoh*
…my money	…el dinero *el deeneroh*
…my keys	…las llaves *las yabais*
…my glasses	…las gafas *las gafas*
My luggage is missing	Se ha perdido mi equipaje *say ah perdeedoh mee ekeepahay*
Has it turned up yet?	¿Ha aparecido ya? *ah ahparetheedoh yah*
My suitcase has been damaged	Mi maleta está estropeada *mee maletah estah aistropeadah*

la cartera
lah karterah
wallet

el monedero
el monaideroh
purse

el maletín
el malaiteen
briefcase

el bolso
el bolsoh
handbag

la maleta
la malaitah
suitcase

el cheque de viaje
el chekay day beeyahay
traveller's cheque

la tarjeta de crédito
lah tarhetah day kredeetoh
credit card

el pasaporte
el pasaportay
passport

la cámara
lah kamarah
camera

el móvil
el mohbeel
mobile phone

I need to phone my insurance company	Tengo que llamar a mi compañía de seguros *taingoh kay yamar ah mee kompanyeeah day segooros*
Can I put a stop on my credit cards?	¿Puedo invalidar mis tarjetas de crédito? *pwedoh eenbaleedar mees tarhetas day kredeetoh*
My name is...	Me llamo... *may yamoh*
My policy number is...	El número de mi póliza es.. *el noomeroh day mee poleethah es*
My address is...	Mi dirección es... *mee deerekthyon es*
My contact number is...	Mi número de contacto es... *mee noomeroh day kontaktoh es*
My email address is...	Mi dirección de email es... *mee deerekthyon day eemaeel es*

MENU GUIDE

This guide lists the most common terms you may encounter on Spanish menus or when shopping for food. If you can't find an exact phrase, then try looking up its component parts.

A

aceitunas olives
acelgas spinach beet
achicoria chicory
aguacate avocado
ahumados smoked
agua mineral mineral water
ajo garlic
al ajillo with garlic
a la parrilla grilled
a la plancha grilled
albaricoques apricots
albóndigas meatballs
alcachofas artichokes
alcaparras capers
al horno baked
allioli garlic mayonnaise
almejas clams
almejas a la marinera clams stewed in wine and parsley
almejas naturales live clams
almendras almonds
almíbar syrup
alubias beans
ancas de rana frogs' legs
anchoas anchovies
anguila eel
angulas baby eels
arenque herring
arroz a la cubana rice with fried eggs and banana fritters
arroz a la valenciana rice with seafood
arroz con leche rice pudding
asados roast meat
atún tuna
azúcar sugar

B

bacalao a la vizcaína cod with ham, peppers, chillies
bacalao al pil pil cod served with chillies and garlic
batido milk shake
bebidas drinks
berenjenas aubergine
besugo al horno baked red bream
bistec de ternera veal steak
bonito fish similar to tuna
boquerones fritos fried fresh anchovies
brazo de gitano swiss roll
brocheta de riñones kidney kebabs
buñuelos fried pastries
butifarra Catalan sausage

C

cabrito asado roast kid
cacahuetes peanuts
cachelada pork stew with eggs, tomato, and onion
café coffee
café con leche coffee with steamed milk
calabacines courgette
calabaza pumpkin
calamares a la romana squid rings in batter
calamares en su tinta squid cooked in their ink
caldeirada fish soup
caldereta gallega vegetable stew
caldo de … … soup
caldo de gallina chicken soup

caldo de pescado clear fish soup

caldo gallego vegetable soup

caldo guanche potato, onion, tomatoes soup

callos a la madrileña tripe cooked with chillies

camarones shrimps

canela cinnamon

cangrejos crabs

caracoles snails

caramelos sweets

carnes meats

castañas chestnuts

cebolla onion

cebolletas spring onions

centollo spider crab

cerdo pork

cerezas cherries

cerveza beer

cesta de frutas selection of fresh fruit

champiñones mushrooms

chanquetes fish (similar to whitebait)

chipirones baby squid

chipirones en su tinta squid cooked in their ink

chocos cuttlefish

chorizo spicy sausage

chuleta de buey beef chop

chuleta de cerdo pork chop

chuleta de cerdo empanada breaded pork chop

chuleta de cordero lamb chop

chuleta de cordero empanada breaded lamb chop

chuleta de ternera veal chop

chuleta de ternera empanada breaded veal chop

chuletas de lomo ahumado smoked pork chops

chuletitas de cordero small lamb chops

chuletón large chop

chuletón de buey large beef chop

churros deep-fried pastry strips

cigalas crayfish

cigalas cocidas boiled crayfish

ciruelas plums

ciruelas pasas prunes

cochinillo asado roast suck ing pig

cocido meat, chickpea, and vegetable stew

cococchas (de merluza) hake stew

cóctel de bogavante lobster cocktail

cóctel de gambas prawn cocktail

cóctel de langostinos jumbo prawn cocktail

cóctel de mariscos seafood cocktail

codornices quail

codornices escabechadas marinated quail

codornices estofadas braised quail

col cabbage

coles de Bruselas Brussels sprouts

coliflor cauliflower

coñac brandy

conejo rabbit

conejo encebollado rabbit with onions

congrio conger eel

consomé con yema consommé with egg yolk

consomé de ave fowl consommé

contra de ternera con guisantes veal stew with peas

contrafilete de ternera veal fillet

copa glass (of wine)

copa de helado ice cream, assorted flavours

cordero asado roast lamb
cordero chilindrón lamb
stew with onion, tomato,
peppers, and eggs
costillas de cerdo pork ribs
crema catalana
crème brûlée
cremada dessert made with
egg, sugar, and milk
crema de… cream of …
soup
crema de legumbres cream
of vegetable soup
crepe imperial crêpe
suzette
criadillas de tierra truffles
crocante ice cream with
chopped nuts
croquetas croquettes
cuajada curds

D, E

dátiles dates
embutidos sausages
embutidos de la tierra local
sausages
empanada gallega fish pie
empanada santiaguesa
fish pie
empanadillas small pies
endivia endive
en escabeche marinated
ensalada salad
ensalada de arenque
fish salad
ensalada ilustrada
mixed salad
ensalada mixta mixed salad
ensalada simple green salad
ensaladilla rusa salad
(potatoes, carrots, peas,
and other vegetables in
mayonnaise)
entrecot a la parrilla grilled
entrecôte
entremeses hors d'oeuvres,
starters
escalope a la milanesa
breaded veal with cheese

escalope a la parrilla
grilled veal
escalope a la plancha
grilled veal
escalope de lomo de cerdo
escalope of pork fillet
escalope de ternera
veal escalope
escalope empanado
breaded escalope
escalopines al vino de
Marsala veal escalopes
cooked in Marsala wine
escalopines de ternera veal
escalopes
espadín a la toledana
kebab
espaguetis spaghetti
espárragos asparagus
espárragos trigueros wild
green asparagus
espinacas spinach
espinazo de cerdo con
patatas stew of pork ribs
with potatoes
estofado braised; stew
estragón tarragon

F

fabada (asturiana) bean
stew with sausage
faisán pheasant
faisán trufado pheasant
with truffles
fiambres cold meats
fideos thin pasta, noodles
filete a la parrilla grilled
beef steak
filete de cerdo pork steak
filete de ternera veal steak
flan crème caramel
frambuesas raspberries
fresas strawberries
fritos fried
fruta fruit

G

gallina en pepitoria chicken
stew with peppers
gambas prawns

gambas cocidas boiled
prawns
gambas en gabardina
prawns in batter
gambas rebozadas prawns
in batter
garbanzos chickpeas
garbanzos a la catalana
chickpeas with sausage,
boiled eggs, and pine nuts
gazpacho andaluz cold
tomato soup
gelatina de … … jelly
gratén de … … au gratin
(baked in a cream and
cheese sauce)
granizado crushed ice drink
gratinada/o au gratin
grelo turnip
grillado grilled
guisantes peas
guisantes salteados
sautéed peas

H
habas broad beans
habichuelas white beans
helado ice cream
helado de vainilla
vanilla ice cream
helado de turrón
nougat ice cream
hígado liver
hígado de ternera
calves' liver
hígado estofado
braised liver
higos con miel y nueces
figs with honey and nuts
higos secos dried figs
horchata (de chufas) cold
drink made from tiger nuts
huevo hilado egg yolk
garnish
huevos eggs
huevos a la flamenca fried
eggs with ham, tomato,
and vegetables
huevos cocidos
hard-boiled eggs

huevos con patatas fritas
fried eggs and chips
huevos con picadillo eggs
with minced meat
huevos duros
hard-boiled eggs
huevos escalfados
poached eggs
huevos pasados por agua
soft-boiled eggs
huevos revueltos
scrambled eggs

J
jamón ham
jamón con huevo hilado
ham with egg yolk garnish
jamón serrano cured ham
jarra de vino wine jug
jerez sherry
jeta pigs' cheeks
judías verdes green beans
judías verdes a la española
bean stew
judías verdes al natural
plain green beans
jugo de… …juice

L
langosta lobster
langosta a la americana
lobster with brandy
and garlic
langosta a la catalana
lobster with mushrooms
and ham in white sauce
langosta fría con mayonesa
cold lobster with
mayonnaise
langostinos king prawns
langostinos dos salsas
king prawns cooked in
two sauces
laurel bay leaves
leche milk
leche frita pudding made
from milk and eggs
leche merengada cold milk
with meringue
lechuga lettuce

lengua de buey ox tongue
lengua de cordero lambs' tongue
lenguado a la romana sole in batter
lenguado meunière floured sole fried in butter
lentejas lentils
lentejas aliñadas lentils in vinaigrette dressing
licores spirits, liqueurs
liebre estofada stewed hare
lima lime
limón lemon
lombarda red cabbage
lomo curado pork sausage
lonchas de jamón sliced, cured ham
longaniza cooked Spanish sausage
lubina sea bass
lubina a la marinera sea bass in a parsley sauce

M

macedonia de fruta fruit salad
mahonesa or mayonesa mayonnaise
Málaga a sweet wine
mandarinas tangerines
manitas de cordero lamb shank
manos de cerdo pigs' feet
manos de cerdo a la parrilla grilled pigs' feet
mantecadas small sponge cakes
mantequilla butter
manzanas apples
mariscos cold mixed shellfish
mariscos del día fresh shellfish
mariscos del tiempo seasonal shellfish
medallones steaks
media de agua half bottle of mineral water
mejillones mussels

mejillones a la marinera mussels in a wine sauce
melocotón peach
melón melon
menestra de legumbres vegetable stew
menú de la casa set menu
menú del día set menu
merluza hake
merluza a la cazuela stewed hake
merluza al ajo arriero hake with garlic and chillies
merluza a la riojana hake with chillies
merluza a la romana hake steaks in batter
merluza a la vasca hake in a garlic sauce
merluza en salsa hake in sauce
merluza en salsa verde hake in parsley and wine sauce
merluza fría cold hake
merluza frita fried hake
mermelada jam
mero grouper (fish)
mero en salsa verde grouper in garlic and parsley sauce
mollejas de ternera fritas fried sweetbreads
morcilla blood sausage
morcilla de carnero mutton blood sausage
morros de cerdo pigs' cheeks
morros de vaca cows' cheeks
mortadela salami-type sausage
morteruelo kind of pâté

N, O

nabo turnip
naranjas oranges
nata cream
natillas cold custard
níscalos wild mushrooms

nueces walnuts
orejas de cerdo pigs' ears

P

paella fried rice with seafood and/or meat
paella castellana meat paella
paella valenciana shellfish, rabbit, and chicken paella
paleta de cordero lechal shoulder of lamb
pan bread
panaché de verduras vegetable stew
panceta bacon
parrillada de caza mixed grilled game
parrillada de mariscos mixed grilled shellfish
pasas raisins
pastel de ternera veal pie
pasteles cakes
patatas a la pescadora potatoes with fish
patatas asadas baked potatoes
patatas bravas potatoes in spicy tomato sauce
patatas fritas chips
patitos rellenos stuffed duckling
pato a la naranja duck in orange sauce
pavo turkey
pavo trufado turkey stuffed with truffles
pecho de ternera breast of veal
pechuga de pollo breast of chicken
pepinillos gherkins
pepino cucumber
peras pears
percebes edible barnacle
perdices a la campesina partridges with vegetables
perdices a la manchega partridges in red wine, garlic, herbs, and pepper

perdices escabechadas marinated partridges
perejil parsley
perritos calientes hot dogs
pescaditos fritos fried fish
pestiños sugared pastries flavoured with aniseed
pez espada swordfish
picadillo de ternera minced veal
pimienta black pepper
pimientos peppers
pimientos a la riojana baked red peppers fried in oil and garlic
pimientos morrones type of bell pepper
pimientos verdes green peppers
piña al gratín pineapple au gratin
piña fresca fresh pineapple
pinchitos/pinchos kebabs, snacks served in bars
pinchos morunos pork kebabs
piñones pine nuts
pisto ratatouille
pisto manchego vegetable marrow with onion and tomato
plátanos bananas
plátanos flameados flambéed bananas
pollo chicken
pollo a la riojana chicken with peppers and chillies
pollo al ajillo fried chicken with garlic
pollo asado roast chicken
pollo braseado braised chicken
pollo en cacerola chicken casserole
pollo en pepitoria chicken in wine with saffron, garlic, and almonds
pollos tomateros con zanahorias young chicken with carrots

pomelo grapefruit
potaje castellano thick broth
potaje de... ... stew
puchero canario casserole of meat, chickpeas, and corn
pulpitos con cebolla baby octopus with onions
pulpo octopus
puré de patatas mashed potatoes, potato purée
purrusalda cod with leeks and potatoes

Q

queso con membrillo cheese with quince jelly
queso de bola Dutch cheese
queso de Burgos soft white cheese
queso del país local cheese
queso de oveja sheep's cheese
queso gallego a creamy cheese
Queso manchego a hard, strong cheese
quisquillas shrimps

R

rábanos radishes
ragú de ternera veal ragoût
rape a la americana monkfish with brandy and herbs
rape a la cazuela stewed monkfish
raya skate
rebozado in batter
redondo al horno roast fillet of beef
rellenos stuffed
remolacha beetroot
repollo cabbage
repostería de la casa cakes that are baked on the premises
requesón cream cheese, cottage cheese

revuelto de... scrambled eggs with...
revuelto de ajos tiernos scrambled eggs with spring garlic
revuelto de trigueros scrambled eggs with asparagus
revuelto mixto scrambled eggs with mixed vegetables
riñones kidneys
rodaballo turbot (fish)
romero rosemary
ron rum
roscas sweet pastries

S

sal salt
salchichas sausages
salchichas de Frankfurt hot dog sausages
salchichón sausage similar to salami
salmón ahumado smoked salmon
salmonetes red mullet
salmonetes en papillote red mullet cooked in foil
salmón frío cold salmon
salmorejo sauce of bread, tomatoes, oil, vinegar, green pepper, and garlic
salpicón de mariscos shellfish in vinaigrette
salsa sauce
salsa bechamel white sauce
salsa holandesa hollandaise sauce
sandía watermelon
sardinas a la brasa barbecued sardines
seco dry
semidulce medium-sweet
sesos brains
sesos a la romana fried brains in batter
sesos rebozados brains in batter
setas mushrooms
sidra cider

sobreasada sausage with cayenne pepper
solomillo fillet steak
solomillo con patatas fillet steak with chips
solomillo de ternera fillet of veal
solomillo de vaca fillet of beef
solomillo frío cold roast beef
sopa soup
sopa castellana vegetable soup
sopa de almendras almond soup
sopa de cola de buey oxtail soup
sopa de gallina chicken soup
sopa del día soup of the day
sopa de legumbres vegetable soup
sopa de marisco fish and shellfish soup
sopa de rabo de buey oxtail soup
sopa mallorquina soup of tomato, meat, and eggs
sopa sevillana fish and mayonnaise soup
soufflé de fresones strawberry soufflé

T

tallarines noodles
tallarines a la italiana tagliatelle
tarta cake
tarta de la casa cake baked on the premises
tarta de manzana apple tart
tencas tench
ternera asada roast veal
tocinillos de cielo a very sweet crème caramel
tomates tomatoes
tomillo thyme
torrijas sweet pastries

tortilla a la paisana vegetable omelette
tortilla a su gusto omelette mace to the customer's wishes
tortilla de escabeche fish omelette
tortilla española Spanish omelette with potato, onion, and garlic
tortilla sacromonte vegetable, brains, and sausage omelette
tortillas variadas assorted omelettes
tournedó fillet steak
trucha trout
trucha ahumada smoked trout
trucha escabechada marinated trout
truchas a la marinera trout in wine sauce
truchas molinera trout meunière (floured trout fried in butter)
trufas truffles
turrón nougat

U, V

uvas grapes
verduras vegetables
vieiras scallops
vino de mesa/blanco /rosado/tinto table/ white/rosé/red wine

Z

zanahorias a la crema creamed carrots
zarzuela de mariscos seafood stew
zarzuela de pescados y mariscos fish and shellfish stew
zumo de ... ...juice

DICTIONARY ENGLISH–SPANISH

The gender of a Spanish noun is indicated by the word for *the*:
el (masculine) and **la** (feminine) or **los** (masculine plural) and
las (feminine plural). Spanish adjectives vary according to the
gender and number of the word they describe. Most ending in
"o" adopt an "a" ending in the feminine form; those ending in
"e" usually stay the same.

A

a un/una
about **más o menos**
about; around **alrededor de**
accident **el accidente**
accident and emergency **las
urgencias**
account number **el número
de la cuenta**
adapter **el adaptador**
address **la dirección**
adult **adulto**
aerobics **el aeróbic**
aeroplane **el avión**
after **después**
afternoon **la tarde**
again **otra vez; de nuevo**
air conditioning **el aire
acondicionado**
air stewardess **la azafata**
air travel **los viajes en avión**
airbag **el airbag**
airmail **por avión**
airport **el aeropuerto**
aisle seat **el asiento
de pasillo**
all **todo**
allergic **alérgico**
almost **casi**
alone **solo**
already **ya**
alright **bien**
ambulance **la ambulancia**
and **y**
ankle **el tobillo**
another; other **otro**
antibiotics **los antibióticos**
anything **algo**
apartment **el apartamento**
appointment **la cita**

April **abril**
apron **el delantal**
arm **el brazo**
arm rest **el apoyabrazos**
armband (for swimming)
el manguito
arrivals hall **el vestíbulo
de llegadas**
arrive (verb) **llegar**
art **el arte**
art gallery **la galería
de arte**
arthritis **la artritis**
artificial sweetener **el
edulcorante artificial**
as (like) **como**
asthma **el asma**
at **en**
audio guide **la guía
en audio**
August **agosto**
Australia **Australia**
automatic ticket machine
la máquina de billetes
autumn **otoño (m)**
awful **espantoso**

B

babysitting **hacer de
canguro**
back (body) **la espalda**
backpack **la mochila**
bad **malo**
badminton **bádminton**
bag (luggage) **la bolsa**
baggage allowance **el
equipaje permitido**
baggage reclaim **la recogida
de equipajes**
baker's **la panadería**

baking tray la bandeja de horno
balcony el balcón
ball el balón; el ovillo; la pelota
ballet el ballet
bandage el vendaje
bank el banco la
bank account la cuenta bancaria
bank holiday el día festivo
bank manager el director del banco
bar el bar
barbecue la barbacoa
barber el barbero
baseball el béisbol
baseball mitt el guante de béisbol
basket el cesto
basketball el baloncesto
bath el baño
bath robe el albornoz
bathroom el cuarto de baño
battery la pila
be (verb) estar; ser
beach la playa
beach ball la pelota de playa
beach towel la toalla de playa
beach umbrella la sombrilla
beautiful hermoso
bed la cama
bee la abeja
before antes de
beginner el principiante
behind detrás de
below debajo de
belt el cinturón
beneath por debajo de
beside al lado de
bicycle la bicicleta
bidet el bidé
big grande
bikini el bikini
bill la cuenta
black negro
blanket la manta
bleeding la hemorragia

blender la licuadora
blood pressure la tensión arterial
blood test el análisis de sangre
blue azul
board: on board a bordo
boarding gate la puerta de embarque
boarding pass la tarjeta de embarque
boat trip la excursión en barco
boat el barco
body el cuerpo
body lotion la loción corporal
bonnet (car) el capó
book el libro
book (verb) reservar
book shop la librería
boot (car) el maletero
boot (footwear) la bota
bottle la botella
bottle opener el abrebotellas
bottom (body) el trasero
bottom el fondo
boutique la boutique
bowl el cuenco
boy el chico
boyfriend el novio
bracelet la pulsera
breakdown la avería
breakfast el desayuno
briefcase el maletín
British británico
brooch el broche
bruise el cardenal
brush el cepillo
bubblebath el baño de burbujas
bucket el cubo
bumper el parachoques
burgle (verb) robar
burn la quemadura
bus el autobús
bus station la estación de autobuses

bus stop la parada de autobús
business class la clase preferente
business negocios
bust el busto
butcher's la carnicería
buy (verb) comprar

C

cabin (boat) el camarote
cable car el teleférico
café la cafetería
calm tranquilo
camera la cámara
camera bag la funda de la cámara
camp (verb) acampar
camping kettle el hervidor de agua para camping
camping stove el hornillo para camping
campsite el camping
can (noun) la lata
can (verb) poder
can opener el abrelatas
Canada Canadá
canoe la canoa
capsule la cápsula
car el coche
car crash el accidente de coche
car park el aparcamiento
car rental el alquiler de coches
car stereo el equipo estéreo del coche
caravan la caravana
caravan site el camping para caravanas
care for (verb) encantar
carry (verb) llevar
cash machine el cajero automático
casino el casino
casserole dish la olla
castle el castillo
catamaran el catamarán
catch (verb) coger
cathedral la catedral

CD el CD
central heating la calefacción central
centre el centro
chair lift el telesilla
change (noun) el cambio
change (verb) cambiar
changing room el probador
channel (TV) el canal
charge (verb) cobrar
cheap barato
check in (airport) facturar
check in (hotel) registrarse
check-out (supermarket) la caja
cheek la mejilla
cheers salud
cheque el cheque
cheque card la tarjeta bancaria
chequebook el talonario de cheques
chest el pecho
chewing gum el chicle
child niño
chin la barbilla
chopping board la tabla de cortar
church la iglesia
cigarette el cigarrillo
cinema el cine
city la ciudad
clean limpio
close (verb) cerrar
closed cerrado
clothes la ropa
cloudy nublado
coast la costa
coat el abrigo
coat hanger la percha
colander el colador
cold (adj) frío
cold (illness) el resfriado
colour el color
colouring pencil el lápiz de colores
come (verb) venir
comic el tebeo
compartment el compartimento

compass la brújula
complain (verb) quejarse
computer el ordenador
concert el concierto
concourse la sala de la estación
conditioner el suavizante
constipation el extreñimiento
consul el cónsul
consulate el consulado
contact number el número de contacto
coolbox la nevera
corkscrew el sacacorchos
cot la cuna
couchette la litera
cough la tos
country el país
courier el mensajero
credit card la tarjeta de crédito
crime la delincuencia
crockery la vajilla
cross trainer la bicicleta elíptica
cufflinks los gemelos
culture la cultura
cup la taza
cut (verb) cortar
cutlery los cubiertos
cycling helmet el casco de ciclista

D

dairy foods los productos lácteos
damaged estropeado
dance (verb) bailar
dashboard el salpicadero
daughter la hija
day el día
December diciembre
deck chair la hamaca
degrees grados
delayed con retraso
delicatessen la charcutería
delicious delicioso
dentist el dentista
deodorant el desodorante

departure board el tablero de anuncios de salidas
departures hall el vestíbulo de salidas
deposit el depósito
desk el mostrador
dessertspoon la cuchara de postre
detergent el detergente
develop (a film) revelar
diabetic diabético
diarrhoea la diarrea
diesel diésel
digital camera la cámara digital
dining car el vagón comedor
dinner la cena
disabled parking el aparcamiento para minusválidos
disabled person la persona minusválida
dish el plato
dive (verb) tirarse
divorced divorciado
do (verb) hacer
doctor el médico
doctor's surgery la consulta del médico
dog el perro
doll la muñeca
door la puerta
double bed la cama de matrimonio
double room la habitación doble
drawing el dibujo
dress el vestido
dressing el aliño
drink (noun) la bebida
drink (verb) beber
drive (verb) conducir
driving licence el carné de conducir
dry seco
during durante
dust pan el recogedor
dustbin el cubo de la basura

duty-free shop la tienda
libre de impuestos
DVD player el reproductor
de DVD

E

each cada
ear la oreja
early temprano
east el este
eat (verb) comer
elbow el codo
electric razor la maquinilla
eléctrica
electrician el electricista
electricity la electricidad
email el email
email address la dirección
de email
embassy la embajada
emergency room la sala
de urgencias
emergency services los
servicios de urgencia
empty vacío
engine el motor
English inglés
engraving el grabado
enjoy (verb) disfrutar
enough bastante
entrance la entrada
envelope el sobre
epileptic epiléptico
equipment el equipamiento
euro el euro
evening la noche
evening dress el traje
de noche
evening meal la cena
every cada
examine (verb) examinar
exchange rate el cambio
excursion la excursión
exercise bike la bicicleta
estática
exhaust (car) el tubo de
escape
exit la salida
expensive caro
experience la experiencia

express service el servicio
rápido
extension lead el alargador
extra extra
eye el ojo

F

face la cara
fairground el parque de
atracciones
family la familia
family room la habitación
familiar
family ticket la entrada
familiar
fan el ventilador
far lejos
fare la tarifa
fast rápido
father el padre
favourite preferido
February febrero
feel (verb) sentir
ferry el ferry
fill (verb) llenar
film (roll of) el carrete
film (cinema) la película
find (verb) encontrar
fine (legal) la multa
finger el dedo
finish (verb) acabar;
terminar
fire alarm la alarma de
incendios
fire brigade los bomberos
fire engine el camión de
bomberos
fire extinguisher el extintor
firefighter el bombero
first primero
fishing pescar
fishmonger la pescadería
fix (verb) arreglar
flash gun el flash
flash photography la
fotografía con flash
flight el vuelo
flight meal la comida
de avión
flip-flops las chanclas

flippers las aletas
float el flotador
flu la gripe
food el alimento; la comida
foot el pie
football el fútbol
for para
forget (verb) olvidar
fork el tenedor
form la forma
fracture la fractura
free (no charge) gratis
free (not engaged) libre
fresh fresco
Friday viernes
fridge-freezer el frigorífico
  congelador
friend el amigo
friendly amable
from de; desde
front delante; in front of
  delante de
frying pan la sartén
fuel gauge el indicador del
  nivel de la gasolina
full lleno
furniture shop la tienda de
  muebles
fuse box la caja de los
  plomos

G

gallery (theatre) el gallinero
game el juego
garage el garaje
garden el jardín
gas el gas
gate la puerta
gear stick el cambio de
  marchas
gift el regalo
gift shop la tienda de
  artículos de regalo
gift-wrap envuelto para
  regalo
girl la chica
girlfriend la novia
give (verb) dar
glass el vaso
glasses las gafas

gloss brillante
go (verb) ir
go clubbing ir de discotecas
goggles las gafas de
  natación
golf el golf
golf ball la pelota de golf
golf club el palo de golf
golf course el campo
  de golf
golf tee el tee de golf
good bien; bueno
good evening buenas tardes
good morning buenos días
goodbye adiós
goodnight buenas noches
grater el rallador
graze el rasguño
Great Britain Gran Bretaña
green verde
greengrocer la verdulería
grill pan la plancha
group el grupo
guarantee la garantía
guest el invitado
guide el guía
guidebook la guía
guided tour el recorrido
  guiado
gym el gimnasio

H

hair el pelo
hairdryer el secador de pelo
half medio/media
half la mitad
hand la mano
hand luggage el equipaje
  de mano
handbag el bolso; la cartera
handle la manilla
handsome guapo
happen (verb) pasar
happy contento; feliz
harbour el puerto
hardware shop la ferretería
hatchback el coche de cinco
  puertas
hate (verb) detestar
have (verb) tener

hayfever la alergia al polen

hazard lights las luces antiniebla

he él

head la cabeza

head rest el reposacabezas

headache el dolor de cabeza

headlight el faro

health la salud

health insurance el seguro médico

hear (verb) oír

heart condition la enfermedad cardíaca

heater la calefacción

heel el talón

hello hola

helmet el casco

help (verb) ayudar

here aquí

high blood pressure la tensión alta

high chair la trona

high-speed train el tren de alta velocidad

hiking el senderismo

hold (verb) sujetar

holdall la bolsa de viaje

holiday las vacaciones; on holiday de vacaciones

home: at home en casa

horn el cláxon

horse riding montar a caballo

hospital el hospital

hot caliente

hotel el hotel

hour la hora

house la casa

hovercraft el aerodeslizador

how many? ¿cuántos?

how? ¿cómo?

humid húmedo

hundred cien

husband el marido

hydrant la boca de riego

hydrofoil el aliscafo

I

I (1st person) yo

ice el hielo

ice cream el helado

icy hielo

ID el documento de identidad

ill enfermo

illness la enfermedad

in en

induction session la sesión de introducción

inhaler el inhalador

injection la inyección

injure (verb) herir; lesionar

insect repellent el repelente de insectos

insurance el seguro

insurance company la compañía de seguros

insurance policy la póliza de seguros

intensive care unit la unidad de cuidados intensivos

interest (verb) interesar

interesting interesante

internet internet

internet café el cibercafé

interpreter el intérprete

inventory el inventario

iPod el iPod

iron la plancha

ironing board la tabla de planchar

it ello; lo/la

J

jacket la haqueta

January enero

jaw la mandíbula

jazz club el club de jazz

jeans los tejanos

jellyfish la medusa

jet ski la moto acuática

jeweller la joyería

jewellery las joyas

journey el viaje

juice el zumo

July julio

jumper el jersey
June junio

K

keep (verb) mantener
kettle el hervidor de agua
key la llave
keyboard el teclado
kidney el riñón
kilo el kilo
kilometre el kilómetro
kitchen la cocina
knee la rodilla
knife el cuchillo
know (a fact) saber
know (people) conocer

L

lake el lago
laptop el portátil
last último
late atrasado; tarde
lawyer el abogado
leak el escape
leave dejar
left la izquierda
left luggage la consigna
leg la pierna
leisure activities los
    pasatiempos
lens la lente
life jacket el chaleco
    salvavidas
lifebuoy el salvavidas
lifeguard el socorrista
lift el ascensor
lift pass el pase para el
    telesilla
light la luz
light (not heavy) ligero
light (verb) encender
light bulb la bombilla
lighter el mechero
lighthouse el faro
like (verb) gustar
list la lista
listen (verb) escuchar
little poco
lock la cerradura
log on (verb) iniciar sesión

log out (verb) cerrar sesión
long largo
look for (verb) buscar
lose (verb) perder
lost property los objetos
    perdidos
love (verb) amar
luggage el equipaje
lunch la comida

M

magazine la revista
make (verb) hacer
mallet el mazo
man el hombre
manual manual
manuscript el manuscrito
many muchos
map el mapa
marina el puerto deportivo
market el mercado
married casado
match (light) la cerilla
match (sport) el partido
mattress el colchón
May mayo
meal la comida
mechanic el mecánico
medicine la medicina
memory card la tarjeta de
    memoria
memory stick llave USB
menu el menú
message el mensaje
microwave el microondas
midday el mediodía
middle el centro
midnight la medianoche
mini bar el minibar
minute el minuto
mistake el error
misty niebla
mixing bowl el bol
mobile phone el móvil
mole (medical) el lunar
Monday lunes
money el dinero
month el mes
monument el monumento
mooring el atracadero

mop la fregona
more más
morning la mañana
mother la madre
motorbike la moto
motorway la autopista
mountain la montaña
mountain bike la bicicleta
  de montaña
mouse (computer) el ratón
mouth la boca
mouthwash el enjuague
  bucal
much mucho
murder el delito
museum el museo
music la música
musician el músico
my mi
myself yo mismo

N

nail la uña
nail clippers los cortaúñas
nail scissors las tijeras para
  las uñas
name el nombre
napkin la servilleta
nausea la naúsea
near cerca
nearby por aquí cerca
neck el cuello
necklace el collar
need (verb) necesitar
never nunca
new nuevo
newsagent la tienda de
  prensa
newspaper el periódico
next próximo
next to cerca de
nice (person) simpático
night la noche
nightclub el club nocturno
no no
north el norte
nose la nariz
nosebleed la hemorragia
  nasal
not no

nothing nada
November noviembre
number el número
nurse la enfermera
nursery slope la pista para
  principiantes

O

October octubre
of de
often con frecuencia
oil el aceite
ointment la pomada
on en
one uno; this one/that one
  éste/ése
only sólo
open (verb) abrir
opening hours el horario
opera la ópera
opera house el teatro de
  la ópera
operation la operación
opposite enfrente de
or o
orange (colour) la naranja
order (verb) pedir
our nuestro
outside fuera
oven el horno
oven gloves las manoplas
  para el horno
over por
over there por allí
owe (verb) deber

P

pain el dolor
painkiller el calmante
painting la pintura
pair el par
paper el papel
papers (identity) la
  documentación; los
  papeles
parcel el paquete
park (noun) el parque
park (verb) aparcar
parking meter el
  parquímetro

passenger el pasajero
passport el pasaporte
passport control el control de pasaportes
pay (verb) pagar
pay in ingresar
pedestrian crossing el paso de peatones
peeler el pelador
pen el bolígrafo
pencil el lápiz
people las personas
perhaps quizás
personal CD player el reproductor personal de CD
pet el animal doméstico
petrol la gasolina
petrol station la gasolinera
pharmacist el farmacéutico
pharmacy la farmacia
phone card la tarjeta telefónica
photo album el álbum de fotos
photo frame el marco para fotos
photograph la fotografía
photography hacer fotos
pianist el pianista
picnic el picnic
picnic hamper la canasta de la comida
piece el trozo de
pilates pilates
pill la pastilla
pillow la almohada
pilot el piloto
PIN el pin
place el lugar
plaster la tirita
plate el plato
platform el andén
play (theatre) representar
pleasant agradable
please por favor
plug (electric) el enchufe
police car el coche patrulla
police station la comisaría
police la policía

policeman el policía
policewoman la mujer policía
policy la póliza
pool: swimming pool la piscina
popcorn las palomitas de maíz
porter el botones
possible posible
post el correo
post office la oficina de correos
postbox el buzón
postcard la postal
postman el cartero
prefer (verb) preferir
pregnant embarazada
prescription la receta
pretty bonito
price el precio
print (photo) la copia
print (verb) imprimir
pump (bicycle) la mancha
puncture el pinchazo
purse el monedero
put (verb) poner

Q, R

quarter el cuarto
quick rápido
quite bastante
radiator el radiador
radio la radio
railway el ferrocarril
raining lloviendo
rape la violación
rash el sarpullido
razor la maquinilla de afeitar
read (verb) leer
ready listo
reboot (verb) reiniciar
receipt el recibo
reclaim tag la etiqueta de identificación de equipaje
recommend recomendar
record shop la tienda de discos

red rojo
reduction el descuento
registration number (car) la matrícula
remote control el mando a distancia
rent (verb) alquilar
repair (noun) la reparación
repair (verb) arreglar
report (noun) la denuncia
report (verb) informar de
reservation la reserva
restaurant el restaurante
restaurant car el vagón restaurante
resuscitation la boca a boca
retired jubilado
return ticket el billete de ida y vuelta
rides las atracciones
right (correct) correcto
right (direction) la derecha
river el río
road la carretera
road signs las señales de tráfico
rob (verb) asaltar
robbery el asalto
roll (of film) el carrete
roofrack la baca
room la habitación
round redondo
roundabout la glorieta
rowing machine la máquina de remo
rubbish bin el cubo de la basura

S

safe seguro
sailing navegar
sailboat el barco de vela
saloon car el turismo
same mismo
sand la arena
sandal la sandalia
satellite TV la televisión por satélite
Saturday sábado
saucepan la cacerola

saucer el plato
say (verb) decir
scan el escáner
scissors las tijeras
scooter la vespa
sea el mar
season la estación
seat el asiento
second (position) segundo
second (time) el segundo
see (verb) ver
sell (verb) vender
sell-by date la fecha de caducidad
send (verb) enviar
senior citizen la persona de la tercera
separately por separado
September septiembre
serious complicado
shampoo el champú
shaving foam la espuma de afeitar
she ella
shirt la camisa
shoe el zapato
shop la tienda
shopping mall el centro comercial
shopping ir de compras
shorts los pantalones cortos
shoulder el hombro
shower la ducha
shower gel el gel de ducha
side effect el efecto secundario
to sign (verb) firmar
signpost señalizar
singer el cantante
single room la habitación individual
single ticket el billete de ida
size (clothes) la talla
size (shoes) el número
ski (verb) esquiar
ski boots las botas de esquí
skin la piel
skirt la falda
skis los esquíes

sleeping bag el saco de dormir

slice la loncha; el trozo

sliproad la vía de acceso

slow lento

small pequeño

smoke (verb) fumar

smoke alarm la alarma de incendios

snack el tentempié

snake la serpiente

sneeze el estornudo

snorkel el tubo de buceo

snow (verb) nevar

snowboard la tabla de snowboard

so tan

soap el jabón

socks los calcetines

soft toy el peluche

some unos

somebody; someone alguien

something algo

sometimes a veces

soon pronto

sorry siento; I'm sorry lo siento

south el sur

souvenir el recuerdo

Spain España

Spanish español

spare tyre la rueda de repuesto

spatula la espátula

speak (verb) hablar

speed limit la velocidad máxima

speedometer el velocímetro

splint la tablilla

splinter la astilla

spoon la cuchara

sport el deporte

sports centre el centro deportivo

sprain el esguince

spring la primavera

square (in town) la plaza

squash (game) el squash

stairs las escaleras

stamp el sello

start (verb) empezar

station (railway) la estación

station (underground) la boca de metro

statue la estatua

stay (verb) quedarse

steering wheel el volante

sterling la libra

sticky tape la cinta adhesiva

stolen robado

stomach el estómago

stomach ache el dolor de estómago

stop! ¡alto!

stop (verb) parar

stopcock la llave de paso

stormy tormenta

street la calle

street map el plano

string el cordel

strong fuerte

student el estudiante

student card el carné de estudiante

suit el traje

suitcase la maleta

summer el verano

sun el sol

sun lounger la tumbona

sunburn la quemadura del sol

Sunday domingo

sunglasses las gafas de sol

sunhat el sombrero

sunscreen la crema con filtro solar

supermarket el supermercado

suppositories los supositorios

surf (verb) hacer surf

surfboard la tabla de surf

sweet dulce

swim (verb) nadar

swimsuit el bañador

T

table la mesa

tablet la pastilla

tailor el sastre
take (verb) tomar
take off (verb) quitarse
takeaway la comida para
  llevar
talk (verb) conversar; hablar
tall alto
taste (verb) probar
taxi el taxi
taxi driver el/la taxista
taxi rank la parada de taxis
teaspoon la cucharilla
  de café
teeth los dientes
telephone el teléfono
telephone box la cabina
television la televisión; el
  televisor
tell (verb) decir
temperature la temperatura
tennis el tenis
tennis ball la pelota de tenis
tennis court la pista de tenis
tennis racquet la raqueta
  de tenis
tent la tienda
terminal la terminal
than que
thank (verb) agradecer
thanks gracias
that ese/esa
their su/sus
them ellos/as
they ellos/as
thief el ladrón
thing la cosa
this éste/esta
throat la garganta
through por
thumb el pulgar
Thursday el jueves
ticket el billete
tide la marea
tight ajustado
time el tiempo; la hora
timetable el horario
tin (can) la lata
to a
tobacco el tabaco
tobacconist el estanco

today hoy
toe el dedo del pie
toilet el aseo
toll peaje (m)
tomorrow mañana
tonight esta noche
too demasiado
too (also) también
toothache el dolor de
  muelas
toothbrush el cepillo de
  dientes
toothpaste el dentífrico
torch la linterna
tour el recorrido; el viaje
tour guide el/la guía
  turístico/a
tourist el turista
tourist information office
  oficina de turismo
towel toalla (f)
town la ciudad
town centre el centro
town hall el ayuntamiento
toy el juguete
traffic jam el atasco
traffic lights el semáforo
train el tren
trainers las bambas
travel (verb) viajar
traveller's cheque el cheque
  de viaje
trolley el carrito
try (verb) intentar
t-shirt la camiseta
Tuesday martes
twin beds dos camas
tyre el neumático)
tyre pressure la presión de
  los neumáticos

U

umbrella el paraguas
underground railway el
  metro
understand comprender
United States Estados
  Unidos
unleaded sin plomo
until hasta

up (not down) arriba
urgent urgente
us nosotros
use (verb) usar
useful útil
usual habitual
usually habitualmente

V

vacancy la habitación libre
vacuum flask el termo
valid válido
valuables los objetos de valor
value el valor
vegetarian vegetariano
vehicle el vehículo
venetian blind la persiana de lamas
very muy; mucho
video game el videojuego
view la vista
village el pueblo
vineyard la viña la
visa la visa (f)
visit visita (f)
visitor visitante (m)

W

wait (verb) esperar
waiter el camarero
waitress la camamera
waiting room la sala de espera
walk (verb) andar
ward la sala
warm caliente; caluroso
washing machine la lavadora
wasp la avispa
watch (verb) mirar
water el agua
waterfall la cascada
we nosotros/as
weather el tiempo
website la página web la
week la semana
well bien
west el oeste
wet húmedo

what? ¿qué?
wheel la rueda
wheelchair access el acceso para sillas de ruedas
wheelchair ramp la rampa para sillas de ruedas
when? ¿cuándo?
where? ¿dónde?
which? ¿qué?; ¿cuál?
whisk el batidor
white blanco
who? ¿quién?
why? ¿por qué?
widescreen TV el televisor de pantalla ancha
wife la esposa
wind el viento
window seat el asiento de ventanilla
windscreen el parabrisas
windscreen wiper el impiaparabrisas
windsurfing hacer windsurf
wine el vino
winter el invierno
with con
without sin
witness el testigo
woman la mujer
work el trabajo
work (verb) trabajar
wrap (gift) envolver
wrist la muñeca
wrist watch el reloj de muñeca
wrong (not right) incorrecto

X, Y, Z

X-ray la radiografía
yacht el yate
year el año
yellow amarillo
yes sí
yesterday ayer
you tú; vosotros
your tu; vuestro
zebra crossing el paso de zebra
zoo el zoo

DICTIONARY SPANISH–ENGLISH

The gender of Spanish nouns is indicated by the abbreviations "m" (masculine) and "f" (feminine). Plural nouns are followed by "m pl" or "f pl". Spanish adjectives vary according to the gender and number of the word they describe. Only the masculine form is shown here. In the feminine form most adjectives ending in "o" adopt an "e" ending and those ending in "e" stay the same.

A

a to
abajo below
abeja (f) bee
abogado (m) lawyer
abonar to pay
abrebotellas (m) bottle opener
abrelatas (m) can opener
abrigo (m) coat
abril April
abrir open
acabar to finish
acampar to camp
accesso (m) access
accidente (m) accident
accidente de coche (m) car crash
aceite (m) oil
acera (f) pavement
adaptador (m) adapter
adiós goodbye
aduana (f) customs
adulto adult
aeróbic (m) aerobics
aerodeslizador (m) hovercraft
aeropuerto (m) airport
afeitarse to shave
agosto August
agradable pleasant
agradecer to thank
agua (m) water
ahora now
airbag (m) airbag
aire acondicionado (m) air conditioning
ajustado tight
alargador (m) extension lead

alarma (f) alarm
alarma de incendios (f) fire alarm
alarma de incendios (f) smoke alarm
albornoz (m) bath robe
álbum de fotos (m) photo album
alergia al polen (f) hayfever
alérgico allergic
aletas (f pl) flippers
algo anything; something
alguien somebody; someone
alimento (m) food
aliño (m) dressing
aliscafo (m) hydrofoil
almohada (f) pillow
almuerzo (m) lunch
alquilar to rent
alquiler de coches (m) car rental
alrededor de about; around
¡alto! stop!
amable friendly
amar to love; to like
ambulancia (f) ambulance
amigo/a (m/f) friend
análisis de sangre (m) blood test
andar to walk
andén (m) platform
animal doméstico (m) pet
año (m) year
antes de before
antibióticos (m pl) antibiotics
antiguo old; ancient
apagar to turn off
aparcamiento (m) car park;

parking
aparcamiento para minusválidos (m)
disabled parking
aparcar to park
apartamento (m) apartment
apoyabrazos (m) arm rest
aquí here
arena (f) sand
arreglar to fix; to mend; to repair
arte (m) art
artritis (f) arthritis
asaltar to rob
asalto (m) robbery
ascensor (m) lift
asiento (m) seat
asiento de pasillo (m) aisle seat
asma (m) asthma
astilla (f) splinter
atracadero (m) mooring
atracciones (f pl) rides
atrasado late
Australia Australia
autobús (m) bus
autopista (f) motorway
avería (f) breakdown
avión (m) aeroplane
ayer yesterday
ayudar to help
azafata (f) air stewardess
azul blue

B

baca (f) roofrack
bádminton (m) badminton
bailar to dance
balcón (m) balcony
ballet (m) ballet
balón (m) ball
baloncesto (m) basketball
bañador (m) swimsuit
banco (m) bank
bandeja de horno (f) baking tray
baño (m) bath; bathroom
baño de burbujas (m) bubblebath
bar (m) bar

barato cheap
barbacoa (f) barbecue
barbero (m) barber
barbilla (f) chin
barca (f) small boat
barca de remos (f) rowing boat
barco (m) boat; ship
barco de recreo (m) pleasure boat
barco de vela (m) sailing boat
bastante enough; quite
bastones (m pl) poles (ski)
beber to drink
béisbol (m) baseball
bicicleta (f) bicycle
bicicleta de montaña (f) mountain bike
bicicleta elíptica (f) cross trainer
bicicleta estática (f) exercise bike
bidé (m) bidet
bien alright; good
bikini (m) bikini
billete de ida (m) single ticket
billete de ida y vuelta (m) return ticket
blanco white
boca (f) mouth
boca a boca (f) resuscitation
boca de metro (f) station (underground)
boca de riego (f) hydrant
bol (m) mixing bowl
bolígrafo (m) pen
bolsa (f) bag (luggage)
bolsa de viaje (f) holdall
bolso (m) handbag
bombero (m) firefighter
bomberos (m pl) fire brigade
bombilla (f) light bulb
bonito attractive; pretty
bordo: a bordo on board
bota (f) boot (footwear)
botas de esquí (f pl) ski boots

bote (m) dinghy
botella (f) bottle
botones (m) porter
boutique (f) boutique
brazo (m) arm
brécol (m) broccoli
brillante gloss
británico British
broche (m) brooch
bronceador (m) suntan
  lotion
brújula (f) compass
buenas noches good night;
  good evening
buenas tardes good evening
bueno good; tasty
buenos días good morning
buscar to look for
busto (m) bust
buzón (m) postbox

C

cabeza (f) head
cabina (f) cabin;
  telephone box
cacerola (f) saucepan
cada each; every
cafetería (f) café; snack bar
caja (f) box; check-out
  (supermarket)
caja de los plomos (f)
  fuse box
cajero automático (m)
  cash machine
calcetines (m pl) socks
calefacción (f) heater
calefacción central (f)
  central heating
caliente warm
calle (f) street
calmado calm (sea)
calmante (m) painkiller
caluroso warm; hot
  (weather)
cama (f) bed
cama de matrimonio (f)
  double bed
cámara (f) camera
cámara de usar y tirar (f)
  disposable camera

cámara digital (f) digital
  camera
camarote (m) cabin (boat)
cambiar to change; to
  replace
cambio (m) change (noun);
  exchange rate
cambio de marchas (m)
  gear stick
camión de bomberos (m)
  fire engine
camisa (f) shirt
camping (m) campsite
camping para caravanas
  (m) caravan site
campo de golf (m) golf
  course
Canadá Canada
canal (m) channel (TV)
canasta (f) basket (in
  basketball)
canasta de la comida (f)
  picnic hamper
cangrejo (m) crab
canoa (f) canoe
cantante (m) singer
capó (m) bonnet
cápsula (f) capsule
cara (f) face
caramelos (m pl) sweets
caravana (f) caravan
cardenal (m) bruise
carné de conducir (m)
  driving licence
carné de estudiante (m)
  student card
carnicería (f) butcher's
caro expensive
carrete (m) roll (of film)
carretera (f) road
carretera principal (f)
  main road
carta (f) letter; menu
  carta de vinos (f) wine list
cartero (m) postman
casa (f) house
casa: en casa at home
casado married
casco de ciclista (m) cycle
  helmet

casi almost
casino (m) casino
castillo (m) castle
catamarán (m) catamaran
catedral (f) cathedral
CD (m) CD
cena (f) dinner
centro (m) centre
centro comercial (m)
  shopping mall
centro deportivo (m)
  sports centre
cepillo (m) brush
cerca near
cerca de next to
cerdo (m) pork
cereza (f) cherry
cerilla (f) match (light)
cerrado closed
cerradura (f) lock
cerrar to close
cerrar sesión to log out
cerveza (f) beer
cesto (m) basket
chaleco salvavidas (m)
  life jacket
champú (m) shampoo
chanclas (f pl) flip-flop
chaqueta (f) jacket
charcutería (f) delicatessen
cheque (m) cheque
chica (f) girl
chicle (m) chewing gum
chico (m) boy
cibercafé (m) internet café
cien hundred
cigarrillo (m) cigarette
cinco five
cine (m) cinema
cinta adhesiva (f)
  sticky tape
cinturón (m) belt
cita (f) appointment
  (arrangement to meet)
ciudad (f) city
clase (f) class; type
clase preferente (f)
  business class
cláxon (m) horn
club de jazz (m) jazz club

club nocturno (m) nightclub
cobrar to charge
coche (m) car
coche de cinco puertas
  (m) hatchback
coche patrulla (m)
  police car
cocina (f) kitchen
codo (m) elbow
coger to catch; to get
colador (m) colander
colchón (m) mattress
collar (m) necklace
color (m) colour
comer to eat
comida (f) food; lunch;
  meal
comida al aire libre (f)
  picnic
comida de avión (f)
  flight meal
comida para llevar (f)
  takeaway
comisaría (f) police station
como as; like; since
¿cómo? how?
compañía de seguros (f)
  insurance company
compartimento (m)
  compartment
complicado serious
comprar to buy
con with
concierto (m) concert
conducir to drive
conocer to know (people)
consigna (f) left luggage
cónsul (m) consul
consulado (m) consulate
consulta del médico (f)
  doctor's surgery
contento happy
contestador automático
  (m) answering machine
control de pasaportes (m)
  passport control
copa (f) glass
copia (f) print (photo)
cordel (m) string
cordero (m) lamb

correcto right (correct)
correo (m) post
corriente (f) current
cortar to cut
cortaúñas (m) nail clippers
costa (f) coast
crema con filtro solar (f) sunscreen
¿cuántos? how many?
cuarto (m) quarter
cuarto de baño (m) bathroom
cuatro four
cubiertos (m pl) cutlery
cubo (m) bucket
cubo de la basura (m) rubbish bin
cuchara (f) spoon
cuchara de postre (f) dessertspoon
cucharilla de café (f) teaspoon
cuchillo (m) knife
cuello (m) neck
cuenco (m) bowl
cuenta (f) bill
cuenta bancaria (f) bank account
cuerpo (m) body
cultura (f) culture
cuna (f) cot

D

dar to give
dato (m) detail
de of; from
debajo de below
deber to owe
decir to say; to tell
decir to tell
dedo (m) finger
dejar to leave
delantal (m) apron
delante front; delante de in front of
delicioso delicious
delincuencia (f) crime
delito (m) crime
dentífrico (m) toothpaste
dentista (m) dentist

dentro inside
denuncia (f) report (noun)
deporte (m) sport
depósito (m) deposit
derecha (f) right (direction)
desayuno (m) breakfast
descuento (m) reduction
desde from
desodorante (m) deodorant
después after
detergente (m) detergent
detestar to hate
detrás de behind
día (m) day
día festivo (m) bank holiday
diabético diabetic
diarrea (f) diarrhoea
dibujo (m) drawing
diciembre December
dientes (m pl) teeth
diésel diesel
diez ten
dinero (m) money
dirección (f) address
dirección de email (f) email address
director del banco (m) bank manager
disfrutar to enjoy
divorciado divorced
documentación (f) papers (identity)
documento de identidad (m) ID
dolor (m) pain
dolor de cabeza (m) headache
dolor de estómago (m) stomach ache
doloroso painful
domingo Sunday
¿dónde? where?
dos two
ducha (f) shower
dulce sweet
durante during

E

edulcorante artificial (m) artificial sweetener
efecto secundario (m) side effect
él he
electricidad (f) electricity
electricista (m) electrician
ella she; her
ello it
ellos/as they; them
email (m) email
embajada (f) embassy
embarazada pregnant
empezar to start
en on; at; in
encantar to care for
encender to light
enchufe (m) plug
encontrar to find
enero January
enfermedad (f) illness
enfermedad cardíaca (f) heart condition
enfermera (f) nurse
enfermo ill
enfrente de opposite
enjuague bucal (m) mouthwash
ensalada (f) salad
entrada (f) entrance; entrance ticket
entrada familiar (f) family ticket
entretenimiento (m) entertainment
enviar to send
envuelto para regalo gift-wrap
epiléptico epileptic
equipaje (m) luggage
equipaje de mano (m) hand luggage
equipaje permitido (m) baggage allowance
equipamiento (m) equipment
equipo estéreo del coche (m) car stereo
error (m) mistake

escaleras (f pl) stairs
escáner (m) scan
escape (m) leak
escuchar to listen
ese/esa that
esguince (m) sprain
espalda (f) back (body)
España Spain
español Spanish
espantoso awful
espátula (f) spatula
esposas (f pl) handcuffs
espuma de afeitar (f) shaving foam
esquiar to ski
esquíes (m pl) skis
estación (f) season
estación de autobuses (f) bus station
estación del tren railway station
estar be (verb)
estatua (f) statue
este (m) east
éste/esta this
estómago (m) stomach
estornudo (m) sneeze
estropeado damaged
estudiante (m) student
etiqueta de identificación de equipaje (f) reclaim tag
euro (m) euro
examinar to examine
excursión (f) excursion
excursión en barco (f) boat trip
experiencia (f) experience
extintor (m) fire extinguisher
extra extra
extreñimiento (m) constipation

F

facturar to check in (at airport)
falda (f) skirt
familia (f) family
farmacéutico (m) pharmacist

farmacia (f) pharmacy
faro (m) headlight; lighthouse
febrero February
fecha de caducidad (f) sell-by date
fecha de caducidad (f) sell-by date
feliz happy
ferretería (f) hardware shop
ferrocarril (m) railway
ferry (m) ferry
fiesta nacional (f) public holiday
filete (m) steak
firmar to sign
flash (m) flash gun
flotador (m) float
folleto (m) leaflet
forma (f) form
fotografía (f) photograph
fotografía con flash (f) flash photography
fractura (f) fracture
frecuencia: con frecuencia often
fregona (f) mop
freír to fry
fresco fresh
frigorífico congelador (m) fridge-freezer
frío cold (adj)
fuera outside
fuerte strong
fumar to smoke
funda de la cámara (f) camera bag
fútbol (m) football

G

gafas (f pl) glasses
gafas de buceo (f pl) mask (swimming)
gafas de natación (f pl) goggles
gafas de sol (f pl) sunglasses
galería de arte (f) art gallery
gallinero (m) gallery (in theatre)

gamba (f) prawn
garaje (m) garage
garantía (f) guarantee
gas (m) gas
gas: con gas sparkling
gasolina (f) petrol
gasolinera (f) petrol station
gel de ducha (m) shower gel
gemelos (m pl) cufflinks
gimnasio (m) gym
glorieta (f) roundabout
golf (m) golf
grabado (m) engraving
gracias thanks
grados degrees
Gran Bretaña Great Britain
granada (f) pomegranate
grande big; large
gratis free (no charge)
gripe (f) flu
grupo (m) group
guante de béisbol (m) baseball mitt
guapo handsome
guarnición (f) side dish
guía (f) guidebook
guía (m) guide
guía en audio (f) audio guide
gustar to like

H

habitación (f) room
habitación doble (f) double room
habitación familiar (f) family room
habitación individual (f) single room
hablar to speak; to talk
hacer to do; to make
hacer de canguro babysitting
hacer fotos photography
hacer la maleta pack
hacer surf to surf
hamaca (f) deck chair
hasta until
hay there is/there are

hemorragia (f) bleeding
hemorragia nasal (f) nosebleed
herida (f) wound; injury
herir injure
hermoso beautiful
hervido boiled
hervidor de agua (m) kettle
hervidor de agua para camping (m) camping kettle
hielo (m) ice; icy (adj)
hígado (m) liver
hija (f) daughter
hogar (m) home
hola hello
hombre (m) man
hombro (m) shoulder
hora (f) hour
horario (m) timetable
horario de apertura (m) opening hours
horario de visitas (m) visiting hours
hornillo para camping (m) camping stove
horno (m) oven
hospital (m) hospital
hotel (m) hotel
húmedo humid

I

iglesia (f) church
imprimir to print
indicador del nivel de la gasolina (m) fuel gauge
informar de to report
inglés English
ingresar pay in
inhalador (m) inhaler
iniciar sesión to log on
interesante interesting
interesar to interest
interior: del interior inland
internet internet
intérprete (m) interpreter
inventario (m) inventory
invierno (m) winter
invitado (m) guest
inyección (f) injection

iPod (m) iPod
ir to go
ir de compras to go shopping
ir de discotecas to go clubbing
izquierda (f) left

J

jabón (m) soap
jardín (m) garden
jersey (m) jumper
joyas (f pl) jewellery
joyería (f) jeweller
jubilado retired
juego (m) game
jugar to play (games)
julio July
junio June

K, L

kilo (m) kilo
kilómetro (m) kilometre
lado: al lado de beside
lago (m) lake
lápiz (m) pencil
lápiz de colores (m) colouring pencil
largo long
lata (f) can (noun)
leer to read
lejos far
lente (f) lens
lento slow
lesionar to injure
libra (f) sterling
libre free (not engaged)
librería (f) book shop
libro (m) book
licuadora (f) blender
ligero light (not heavy)
limpiador/a (m/f) cleaner
limpio clean
lista (f) list
listo ready
litera (f) couchette
llamada (f) phone call
llanta (f) tyre
llave (f) key
llave de paso (f) stopcock

llave USB (f) memory stick
llegar to arrive; to come
llenar to fill
lleno full
llevar to bring; to carry; to wear
lloviendo raining
lo/la it
loción corporal (f) body lotion
loncha (f) slice
luces (f pl) lights
luces antiniebla (f pl) hazard lights
lugar (m) place
lunar (m) mole (medical)
lunes Monday
luz (f) light

M

madre (f) mother
maleta (f) suitcase
maletero (m) boot (car)
maletín (m) briefcase
malo bad
mañana (f) morning
mañana tomorrow
mancha (f) pump (bicycle)
mandar to send
mandíbula (f) jaw
mando a distancia (m) remote control
manguito (m) armband (for swimming)
manilla (f) handle
manillar (m) handlebars
mano (f) hand
manoplas para el horno (f pl) oven gloves
manta (f) blanket
mantener to keep; to maintain
manual manual
manuscrito (m) manuscript
mapa (m) map
máquina (f) machine
máquina de billetes (f) automatic ticket machine
máquina de remo (f) rowing machine

maquinilla de afeitar (f) razor
maquinilla eléctrica (f) electric razor
mar (m) sea
marco para fotos (m) photo frame
marido (m) husband
marisco (m) seafood
más more
más o menos about
matrícula (f) number plate; registration number
mayo May
mazo (m) mallet
mecánico (m) mechanic
mechero (m) lighter
medianoche (f) midnight
medicina medicine
médico (m) doctor
medio/media half
mediodía (m) midday
medusa (f) jellyfish
mejilla (f) cheek
mensaje (m) message
mensajero (m) courier
menú (m) menu
mercado (m) market
mes (m) month
mesa (f) table
mi my
microondas (m) microwave
minibar (m) mini bar
minuto (m) minute
mirar to watch
mismo same
mitad (f) half
mixto mixed
mochila (f) backpack
monedero (m) purse
montaña (f) mountain
montar a caballo to go horse riding
monumento (m) monument
mostrador (m) desk
moto (f) motorbike
moto acuática (f) jet ski
motor (m) engine
móvil (m) mobile phone

mucho much
muchos many
mujer policía (f) policewoman
multa (f) fine (legal)
muñeca (f) doll
museo (m) museum
música (f) music
músico (m) musician

N

nada nothing
nadar to go swimming
naranja (f) orange (colour)
nariz (f) nose
nata (f) cream
natación swimming
naúsea (f) nausea
navegar sailing
necesitar to need
negocios business
negro black
nevar to snow
nevera (f) coolbox
niebla misty;
niño child
no no; not
noche (f) evening; night
nombre (m) name
norte (m) north
noviembre November
novio/a (m/f) boy/girlfriend
nublado cloudy
nuestro our
nueve nine
nuevo new;
  de nuevo again
número (m) number; size (shoes)
número de contacto (m) contact number
número de la cuenta (m) account number
nunca never

O

o or
objetos perdidos (m pl) lost property
octubre October

oficina de correos (f) post office
oír to hear
ojo (m) eye
olla (f) casserole dish
olvidar to forget
ópera (f) opera
operación (f) operation
ordenador (m) computer
oreja (f) ear
otoño (m) autumn
otra vez again
otro another; other
ovillo (m) ball

P

padre (m) father
pagar to pay
país (m) country
palo de golf (m) golf club
panadería (f) baker's
panecillo (m) bread roll
pantalones cortos (m pl) shorts
papel (m) paper
papeles (m pl) papers (identity)
paquete (m) package; packet; parcel
par (m) pair
para for
parabólica (f) satellite dish
parachoques (m) bumper
parada de autobús (f) bus stop
parada de taxis (f) taxi rank
parar to stop
parque (m) park (noun)
parque de atracciones (m) fairground
parquímetro (m) parking meter
partido (m) match (sport)
pasajero (m) passenger
pasaporte (m) passport
pasar to happen
pasatiempos (m pl) leisure activities
pase para el telesilla (m) lift pass

paso de peatones (m)
pedestrian crossing
paso de zebra (m) zebra
crossing
pastilla (f) pill; tablet
peaje (m) toll
pecho (m) chest
pedir to order
pelador (m) peeler
película (f) film
pelo (m) hair
pelota (f) ball
pelota de golf (f) golf ball
pelota de playa (f)
beach ball
pelota de tenis (f)
tennis ball
peluche (m) soft toy
pensar to think
pensión (f) guesthouse
pensionista (m/f) senior
citizen
pequeño small
percha (f) coat hanger
perder to lose; to miss
periódico (m) newspaper
pero but
perro (m) dog
persona (f) person
persona de la tercera (f)
senior citizen
persona minusválida (f)
disabled person
personas (f pl) people
pescadería (f) fishmonger
pescar fishing
pianista (m) pianist
picante spicy
pie (m) foot
piel (f) skin
pierna (f) leg
pila (f) battery
pilates pilates
piloto (m) pilot
pin (m) PIN
piña (f) pineapple
pinchazo (m) puncture
pintura (f) painting
piqueta (f) tent peg
piscina (f) swimming pool

piscina descubierta (f)
outdoor pool
pista de tenis (f) tennis
court
pista para principiantes (f)
nursery slope
plancha (f) grill pan; iron
plano (m) street map
platillo (m) saucer
plato (m) dish; plate
playa (f) beach
plaza (f) square (in town)
poco a little
poder can (verb)
policía (f) police
policía (m) policeman
póliza (f) policy
póliza de seguros (f)
insurance policy
pomada (f) ointment
poner to put
por over
por allí over there
por aquí cerca nearby
por avión airmail
por debajo de beneath
por favor please
por separado separately
portátil (m) laptop
posible possible
postal (f) postcard
postre (m) dessert
precio (m) price
preferido favourite
preferir to prefer
primavera (f) spring
primero first
principiante (m) beginner
probador (m) changing
room
programa (m) programme
pronto soon
próximo next
puerta (f) door; gate
puerta de embarque (f)
boarding gate
puerto (m) harbour
puerto deportivo (m)
marina
pulsera (f) bracelet

Q

que than
quedarse to stay
quejarse to complain
quemadura (f) burn
quemadura del sol (f)
  sunburn
quince fifteen
quitarse to take off
quizás perhaps

R

radiador (m) radiator
radio (f) radio
rallador (m) grater
rápido fast; quick
raqueta de tenis (f) tennis
  racquet
rasguño (m) graze
ratón (m) mouse
  (computer)
receta (f) prescription
recibo (m) receipt
recogedor (m) dust pan
recogida de equipajes (f)
  baggage reclaim
recomendar recommend
recorrido guiado (m)
  guided tour
recuerdo (m) souvenir
redondo round
regalo (m) gift; present
registrarse check in (hotel)
reiniciar to reboot
reparación (f) repair (noun)
repelente de insectos (m)
  insect repellent
reposacabezas (m)
  head rest
representar play (theatre)
reproductor de DVD (m)
  DVD player
reproductor personal
  de CD (m) personal CD
  player
reraso: con retraso delayed
reserva (f) reservation
reservar to book; reserve
resfriado (m) cold (illness)
restaurante (m) restaurant

revelar to develop (a film)
revista (f) magazine
río (m) river
robado stolen
robar to burgle
rodilla (f) knee
rojo red
ropa (f) clothes
rosa pink
rueda de repuesto (f)
  spare tyre

S

sábado Saturday
saber to know (a fact)
sacacorchos (m) corkscrew
saco de dormir (m)
  sleeping bag
safari (m) safari park
sala de la estación (f)
  concourse
sala de urgencias
  emergency room
salida (f) exit
salir to go out
salpicadero (m) dashboard
salud cheers
salud (f) health
salvavidas (m) lifebuoy
sandalia (f) sandal
sarpullido (m) rash
sartén (f) frying pan
sastre (m) tailor
secador de pelo (m)
  hairdryer
seco dry
segundo second (position)
segundo (m) second (unit
  of time)
seguro safe
seguro (m) insurance
seguro médico (m) health
  insurance
sello (m) stamp
señales de tráfico (f pl)
  road signs
señalizar signpost
senderismo (m) hiking
sentarse to sit
sentir to feel

septiembre September
ser be (verb)
serpiente (f) snake
servicio rápido (m) express service
servicios de urgencia (m pl) emergency services
servilleta (f) napkin
servir to serve
siento sorry; lo siento I'm sorry
simpático nice (person)
sobre (m) envelope
socorrista (m) lifeguard
sol (m) sun
solo alone
sólo only
soltero single (not married)
sombrero (m) sunhat
sombrilla (f) beach umbrella
squash (m) squash (game)
stepper (m) step machine
su his/her/its/their/your
suavizante (m) conditioner
sujetar to hold
supermercado (m) supermarket
supositorios (m pl) suppositories
sur (m) south
surfing (m) surfing

T

tabaco (m) tobacco
tabla de cortar (f) chopping board
tabla de planchar (f) ironing board
tabla de snowboard (f) snowboard
tabla de surf (f) surfboard
tablero de anuncios de salidas (m) departure board
tablilla (f) splint
talla (f) size (clothes)
talón (m) heel (body)
talonario de cheques (m) chequebook
también too (also)

tan so
tarde late
tarde (f) afternoon
tarifa (f) fare
tarjeta bancaria (f) cheque card
tarjeta de crédito (f) credit card
tarjeta de embarque (f) boarding pass
tarjeta de memoria (f) memory card
tarjeta telefónica (f) phone card
taxi (m) taxi
taza (f) cup
teatro de la ópera (m) opera house
tebeo (m) comic
teclado (m) keyboard
tee de golf (m) golf tee
tejanos (m pl) jeans
teleférico (m) cable car
teléfono (m) telephone
telesilla (f) chair lift
televisión por satélite (f) satellite TV
televisión; el televisor (f) television
temperatura (f) temperature
temprano early
tenedor (m) fork
tener have (verb)
tenis (m) tennis
tensión alta (f) high blood pressure
tensión arterial (f) blood pressure
tentempié (m) snack
terminal (m) terminal
terminar to finish
ternera (f) beef
tienda (f) shop; store; tent
tienda de artículos de regalo (f) gift shop
tienda de discos (f) record shop
tienda de muebles (f) furniture shop

tienda libre de impuestos (f) duty-free shop

tijeras (f pl) scissors

tijeras para las uñas (f pl) nail scissors

tirarse dive

tirita (f) plaster

toalla de playa (f) beach towel

tobillo (m) ankle

todo all

todo recto straight on

tormenta: hay tormenta stormy; it's stormy

tos (f) cough

traje (m) suit

traje de noche (m) evening dress

tranquilo calm (person)

trasero (m) bottom (body)

treinta thirty

tren de alta velocidad (m) high-speed train

tres three

trona (f) high chair

trozo de (m) piece

tubo de buceo (m) snorkel

tubo de escape (m) exhaust (car)

tumbona (f) sun lounger

turismo (m) saloon car

U

último last

un/una a

uña (f) nail

unidad de cuidados intensivos (f) intensive care unit

uno/una one

unos some

urgencias (f pl) accident and emergency department

V

vacaciones (f pl) holiday de vacaciones on holiday

vacío empty

vagón comedor (m) dining car

vagón restaurante (m) restaurant car

vajilla (f) crockery

válido valid (ticket)

valor (m) value

vaso (m) glass

veces: a veces sometimes

vegeteriano vegetarian

veinte twenty

vela (f) sailing

velocidad máxima (f) speed limit

velocímetro (m) speedometer

vendaje (m) bandage

vender to sell

venir to come

ventana (f) window

ventilador (m) fan

ver to see

verano (m) summer

verde green

verdulería (f) greengrocer

vespa (f) scooter

vestíbulo de llegadas (m) arrivals hall

vestíbulo de salidas (m) departures hall

vestido (m) dress

vía de acceso (f) sl proad

viajar to travel

viernes Friday

violación (f) rape

volante (m) steering wheel

volar to fly

vuelo (m) flight

Y

y and

ya already

yate (m) yacht

yo I (1st person)

yo mismo myself

Z

zanahoria (f) carrot

zapato (m) shoe

zoo (m) zoo

zumo (m) juice

ACKNOWLEDGMENTS

Dorling Kindersley would like to thank the following for their help in the preparation of this book: Elma Aquino and Mandy Earey for design assistance; Nicola Hodgson for editorial assistance; Claire Bowers, Lucy Claxton, and Rose Horridge in the DK Picture Library; Adam Brackenbury, Vânia Cunha, Almudena Diaz, Maria Elia, John Goldsmid, Sonia Pati, Phil Sergeant, and Louise Waller for DTP assistance.

PICTURE CREDITS

Key: a (above); b (below/bottom); c (centre); l (left); r (right); t (top)

Alamy Images: Justin Kase zfivez p111cb; PhotoSpin, Inc p36 crb;
Courtesy of Renault: p24–25 t;
Getty Images: Reggie Casagrande p146;
PunchStock: Moodboard p6

Jacket images: *Front:* Corbis: Hugh Sitton/zefa c. *Back:* Corbis: Jeremy Horner

All other images © **Dorling Kindersley**
For further information, see: **www.dkimages.com**